GETTING
MORE
OUT OF
CHURCH

14168181

3/04/6/Prooketon/3.57

BV
4509.5
.K5
1986

GETTING
MORE
OUT OF
CHURCH

WAYNE KISER

**VICTOR
BOOKS** a division of SP Publications, Inc.
WHEATON. ILLINOIS 60187

Offices also in
Whitby, Ontario, Canada
Amersham-on-the-Hill, Bucks, England

Scripture quotations in this book, unless
otherwise noted, are from the *Good News
Bible*—Old Testament: © American Bible
Society 1976; New Testament: © American
Bible Society 1966, 1971, 1976. Other
quotations are from the *King James Version*
(KJV); *The Living Bible* (TLB), © 1971, by
Tyndale House Publishers, Wheaton, Illinois.
Used by permission; the *Holy Bible, New
International Version* (NIV), © 1973, 1978,
1984, International Bible Society. Used by
permission of Zondervan Bible Publishers.

Recommended Dewey Decimal Classification: 248.2
Suggested Subject Heading: RELIGIOUS EXPERIENCE

Library of Congress Catalog Card Number: 85-62702
ISBN: 0-89693-530-2

© 1986 by SP Publications, Inc. All rights reserved
Printed in the United States of America

No part of this book may be reproduced without
written permission, except for brief quotations in
books, critical articles, and reviews.

VICTOR BOOKS
A division of SP Publications, Inc.
Wheaton, Illinois 60187

CONTENTS

42282

The Library
INTERNATIONAL CHRISTIA
GRADUATE UNIVERSITY

PREFACE

The person new to Christianity and the church somehow feels the glow of that experience will never end. But there comes a time when, for many of us, it does end—a time when familiarity with people, routine, unaddressed nagging questions, and other interests, take the edge off that glow. Because we love God and His Son Jesus Christ, we want more from our church experience. We know there must be more, but we don't know how to find it.

After thirty years of faithfully attending churches or serving in pastoral roles, I too came to this spot. And as I talked to others, I found I was not alone. Many of my fellow Christians were facing the same dilemma. It is for these that this book is written.

I have attempted to do more than recite my progress or vent my dissatisfaction. I have tried to offer them a practical guide out of their unhappiness and into an experience which fills their lives with renewed enthusiasm. I trust that the reading of this book will make better church members as they, like I, learn that we get more from church when we give more to it.

I wish to thank my wife, Ruth Ann, who has been my partner in this journey. I have often felt that without her there would be no one to keep me on track, to help me think through issues which are sometimes traumatic for us both, and to come to conclusions that do not sever contacts with the church. She not only pored over manuscripts for many hours, but also contributed much of the thinking that makes up these pages.

Wayne Kiser
Glen Ellyn, Illinois
1986

CHAPTER ONE

When the Joy Is Gone

When I awoke that Sunday morning and prepared for church, I was not thinking about the Sunday School lesson, the sermon, or worshiping the Lord. I was asking myself, "Why do I go through this? Today is going to be the same as it is every Sunday. I'm bored, tired of poor sermons, and sick of the meaningless ritual!"

But I headed for the church much as a drunk heads for his tavern. I knew that I needed something, and I returned to the familiar, despite its shortcomings.

Looking back, I realize I had reached one of the lowest points in my church experience, and perhaps in my Christian life. Remembering happier times only made matters worse. I thought of when I received Christ as my Saviour, and how from that time on, He had been so dear to me. I thought of other Christians I had held in esteem.

I had wanted to serve Christ so much then . . . . I remembered a basketball game where I sat in the bleachers and first felt the burden of the crowd, so many lost and headed for hell without Christ. I wanted to shout the plan of salvation and give an altar call right there.

I remembered early preaching experiences. While I was in high school, a woman from the church I attended obtained permission to use an empty, one-room schoolhouse for religious education. She gathered around her a bunch of country kids and taught them the Bible. I spoke after her lesson because she wanted the kids to have a worship experience and she didn't feel women should preach. Now I know that she did it for my benefit more than hers.

I thought of the day I was ordained and how that infused new vigor into my ministry as a pastor. And there were Sunday School classes, counseling sessions, and a brief career as a missionary. So, you may understand the guilt and frustration I had over my bad attitude. Still, nothing changed the fact that I didn't want to go to church anymore.

If the feeling had come on me all at one time, I would have excused it as the result of something I ate. But it didn't. My attitude had worsened over time. Perhaps you remember the Lone Ranger radio programs. They began, "From out of the past come the thundering hoofbeats of the great horse, Silver." The clop, clop, clop of the hooves kept getting louder until you couldn't ignore them any longer. So it was with my unhappiness about the church.

Years of sameness in the service order, the triteness of my own preaching and the preaching of others, the many unchristian acts of fellow believers, and the ever-growing list of unanswered questions that haunted my Christian experience had finally taken their toll. It was time for a long, hard look at myself and my church. I was ready for a change in my outlook, and I determined that the church in concept and its people in particular were going to mean something to me, as they did many years ago, or I was going to know the reason why.

Though some churches seem to be getting along as well as they ever did, I have found that many members today are going through a church relationship crisis. A man in Indiana left an independent Bible Church of which he had been a member for more than fifty years, because he was singled out by his friends as a troublemaker. He developed a bitter attitude toward the church. A Nazarene couple dropped out of a church in Michigan because, as they said, they "didn't feel comfortable anymore." A Baptist woman in Minnesota resigned her church membership with a scathing letter, frustrated over a minor problem in the youth group. Stories abound from Presbyterians, Methodists, Baptists, and members of almost every denomination who fail to find their churches meaningful any longer. They are waking up and saying to themselves, "There must be more to church than this."

Just being unhappy with the church would be bad enough, but most of these people are trying to solve their dissonance by cutting off the very institution which God ordained to be a supportive influence. Running away is no answer, but many people do it, just the same.

Disenchanted church members often tailor their activities to reflect the fact that the church is no longer meeting their needs. One family man whom I know loads up his camper each summer weekend and heads for a lake. With his wife and children, he attends a vacation church on Sunday mornings. He is doing so to escape an unpleasant situation in his home church. When the church of which he is a member asks him to take part, he says, "You know us. We are gone so much that we can't get involved."

I know of another man who was so unhappy with his minister that the Sunday services were beginning to upset him. He took a job as a teacher in children's church so that he would not have to listen to the pastor. People said, "You are indeed sacrificing your own spiritual growth to serve these little ones. God will reward you." He knew better. Because he was unhappy, he was avoiding contact with what disturbed him.

Many disenchanted members drop out altogether and replace the church with other interests. Though they still consider themselves Christians, they give the church less and less time. The first to go is prayer meeting, then Sunday evening services, then social events; but eventually it comes to Sunday morning.

Dropping out of church activity is not limited to people who have held church membership for years. New Christians can face the problem too. Harry and Ethel fit that pattern. My wife and I first met them at a Sunday School function, shortly after they came to Christ and joined the church. They were a nice couple, the kind we liked to be with, even though their lifestyle was quite different from ours. Then it happened. Domestic problems began to wedge them apart, and when they needed the church the most, it responded the least. That was seven years ago. Recently we met Ethel, now a waitress in a franchise restaurant. She looked much older and worn. A year ago, we had a chance meeting with Harry, who now had a new wife much younger than himself. Harry and Ethel not only separated from one another, but also from the church.

WHAT CAUSES THE UNHAPPINESS?

Because the problem of disenchantment is both complex and subjective, it may be hard to assign a cause. It is much like suffering from a cold or the flu. You may think you became sick from walking in the rain, working long hours, or from personal stress. You only know that you are sick and hurting and will do almost anything to feel better.

If you are unhappy and see yourself withdrawing from your church, you need to take a look at what is happening to you. Here are some of the reasons people point to for their dissatisfaction.

Boredom. Unfortunately, the programs in many churches are a rerun of the year before. The philosophy seems to be, "Once you have found a good method, stick with it."

In highly liturgical worship, the routine is evident. But even in less formal settings, patterns of worship become ingrained. Through constant repetition, the meaningful can become commonplace. The communion service has deep significance for most church members; but who has not experienced at least one service of just going through the motions, rather than really worshiping?

Likewise, keeping the same pattern each Sunday in the service itself can become routine. We follow others as they pray. We sing on cue and contribute to the offering when it is expected. We passively listen to the sermon and experience little personal involvement in the service. The program can seem choreographed and its repetition may cause boredom. For many church members who want meaningful interaction and personal activity, the way they worship is a disappointment.

Is it any wonder that this is the heyday of television preachers? They offer much of what the church does, and in the comfort of the parishioner's living room, just steps away from the refrigerator.

On the other hand, a boring church life has actually helped a few members, for it has been the impetus to drive them into leadership or into other parts of the church program. One pastor who had been a layperson in a local church, told me he had accepted the call to preach at a small mission church. "Rather than just sit here," he said, "I may as well preach."

Activity and the Weight of Responsibility. A person who becomes active in a church to escape boredom may face another problem. Overzealous leaders are willing to sign up any member who either won't or can't say no. He can find himself scheduled so tightly that church meetings and programs become a point of contention with his family and friends. As one lay person said, "Our church keeps us running from meeting to meeting when all we really want is to be involved in a meaningful outreach."

Red Tape. Especially in large churches, just doing the simplest of jobs can be exasperating if you get caught in the bureaucracy. I was teaching a Sunday School class and needed an overhead projector. I called one person, who referred me to another, who sent me to the church secretary, who gave me the proper form, which told me who had the key to the audiovisual room. But the key keeper told me he didn't have the authority to let me use the equipment—and so it went. I decided it would be easier to use the chalkboard, but it took some of the fun out of the session for me.

Frustrated Expectations. A student in a communications class I teach at Wheaton College faced a particularly difficult assignment. In the process of redoing his work for the third time, he wistfully said, "You know, I really looked forward to taking this course." I knew he was having second thoughts about his involvement.

When one expects a pleasant experience in the church and finds that it is a lot of work with little acclaim, he either reassesses his expectations or gets discouraged.

Unhappiness with the Sermons. The quality of sermons varies substantially. In churches where pastors use textbook illustrations, irrelevant issues, and poor logic, parishioners are likely to list those sermons among the reasons why church has lost its excitement. When a person is first converted and Christianity is new to him, almost anything will do in sermons; but as he grows older in the faith, he may come to the place where he feels he has heard it all before.

On the other hand, some pastors use excellent logic and deal with important issues, but tend to speak in theological language that is not understood by their congregations. It is indeed a difficult assignment for a pastor to present relevant and heavy truth in a manner people can understand and relate to. But after all, Jesus said, "Feed My sheep." He didn't say, "Feed My giraffes."

Unhappiness with the Pastor. In most churches, the pastor is more than the person who presents the sermon or officiates in the liturgy. He is usually the central figure in the church and is responsible for many of the decisions which the church makes. Sometimes his personality alone has a great effect.

A pastor in a denominational church in Indiana was expelled because of a mannerism to which the congregation

14

took offense. When he spoke from the pulpit, he scratched his stomach. That gesture so irritated the people that they began to find fault with almost everything he did. Eventually they asked him to leave.

In a Bible Church in Illinois, a man became unhappy with his pastor. As a major contributor and prominent board member, he decided to withhold his giving and boycott the evening service in protest. As others in the church came to him to ask why he was not at the services, he had opportunity to tell his story, rally support for his feelings, and begin a movement to remove the pastor. As a neutral board member explained it to me, "Nothing more than a conflict of personality was to blame. Yet, over this, a whole church split."

If a pastor is out of fellowship with the Lord, the implications may filter through to the people of the congregation and make them feel uncomfortable. United Methodist pastor, Donald Kline, writing in *Good News* Magazine, tells how he had been pastoring churches for thirteen years, but he had never asked Jesus Christ to be "his personal Lord and Saviour." Problems in counseling and tension in the church caused him to consider the root issues of his ministry. Ultimately, he prayed with two other men and asked Christ to be his Saviour. "The heart change God made in me was dramatic. I experienced the lifting of years of pent-up anger and inner emptiness."[1]

He found himself spending more time in the Scriptures and caring more for the people of his congregation. "The results were immediate," he says. "Individuals began to make their own commitments to Christ. Families were restored. A renewal came to our church that was to last with some intensity for more than six years. During that period, outreach giving more than quadrupled. The attendance grew and more importantly, what had been a spiritually cold church became a church on fire for Jesus Christ."

Mid-Life Crisis. Not all the unhappiness within a church is the result of the church structure, its programs, or personalities in conflict. For some members the crisis is personal and internal.

Many people experience changing attitudes toward the church when they enter the time known as mid-life crisis. This is that frightening time when men grow bald and remember the good times that were. It's the time when women begin to sag in the wrong places and wonder why the romance has gone from their lives. Some are tempted to use anything that will tighten the wrinkles, even though they know that, as for Cinderella, the magic will disappear for them too at the stroke of midnight, and they will have to face themselves as they truly are.

I attributed part of my frustration with the church to being in my forties. I could tell by the things I was doing and the questions I was asking myself that I was growing unsettled. "What have I accomplished with my life? What kind of impact have I made for Christ in the world? Why can't I do as much as I used to?"

The real clincher came when I bought an old car. Not just any car, but a 1952 Studebaker—a well-rusted, Bondo bucket, for which some former owner had lovingly sewed quilt block seatcovers. The old car was a piece of my past. To restore it was an admission that my life had changed and I wasn't comfortable in it anymore.

Dissension. Internal conflicts cause tensions which affect all the members, but especially those who are trying to find where they fit into the church. "I not only see churches splitting more today than in the past," says Russell Shive, general director of the Conservative Baptist Association, "but I see them splitting for more reasons. Splits used to be over doctrine," he says, "but now it's mostly over personalities that clash. It can take a full generation for a church to recover from a split."

This kind of infighting discourages members. It is inconsistent with what it means to be a Christian. Many people will withdraw from the church rather than face this kind of tension.

WHAT IF THE PROBLEM GOES UNCHECKED?

Although a growing number of people need to rediscover the church in their personal lives, others are perfectly content with their experience. For them, the church's programs do what they want them to do—draw them before the throne of God, support their Christian lives, and affirm that they are on the right track in the way they live. They are happy, content, and praising God. "The people in this church," said one man, "are like family to me. I look forward to coming to each meeting and taking part in the activities of the church. This is the most fulfilling part of my life."

Unfortunately, those who expect their church relationship to be ideal, when it isn't, can suffer from guilt, and guilt tends to lead to criticism both of themselves and those around them. The eagle-eyed, needle-nosed, nit-picking church member has all but become a legend. One suspicious woman said, "Even if the pastor preached the truth, I probably wouldn't believe him."

I often think of the words of Paul to the church at Philippi: "I urge you, then, to make me completely happy by having the same thoughts, sharing the same love, and being one in soul and mind. Don't do anything from selfish ambition or from a cheap desire to boast, but be humble toward one another, always considering others better than yourselves. And look out for one another's interests, not just for your own. The attitude you should have is the one that Jesus Christ had" (Phil. 2:2-5)

To the church at Colosse Paul wrote, "Be tolerant with one another and forgive one another whenever any of you has a complaint against someone else" (Col. 3:13). Usually those who suffer from our guilt and criticism have done the least to deserve such treatment.

Not only will we experience more tension in the church in the future, if we fail to bring back the joy that once marked our Christian lives, but we are likely to see church rolls continue to decline.

Most pastors and church administrators believe you can't build a church without a core of excited, evangelizing members. Unchecked unhappiness soon yields apathy and stifles witness. In his book, *I Hate Witnessing*, Dick Innes writes,

> I had spent several years training for Christian work. I had pastored a church and was now the director of a Christian organization whose work was evangelism. But I had a big problem and needed to tell God about it. "God," I nervously prayed, "I know that as a Christian and especially as a Christian minister I'm supposed to be doing a lot of witnessing for You. But I'm sick to death of witnessing for You out of a sense of duty and trying to tell others about You because that's what I'm supposed to do. I hate witnessing and I'm quitting!"[2]

Innes spends the rest of the book helping his readers develop a lifestyle which will let their witness flow naturally because they are happy with themselves and their relationship to God's people. If we are not happy with the church, we will not witness for its Lord.

Church life doesn't have to be dull, drab, and grey. We don't have to be discouraged and discontent with ourselves. We don't have to become critical and withdraw our fellowship. God has chosen for the believer to be a celebrant at the feast, to enjoy Him and the brothers and sisters in the faith. The last thing God wants is for the believer to be discouraged with the church.

A church will change as the members take on a new positive attitude toward it. Edmund Robb, Jr. writing in the *Good News* magazine, says that when a church experiences revival, "The Scriptures will be proclaimed, studied, and obeyed . . . there will be an openness to the Holy Spirit . . . laymen will not be satisfied just to pass the offering plate and pay the bills . . . evangelism will be the primary task . . . worship will be central . . . there will be a prophetic voice in the pulpit, and . . . biblical morality will be proclaimed."[3]

Your church reflects your satisfaction and commitment; your church is a barometer of your happiness. If you think that you could stand to improve your enthusiasm, you may want to mark this checklist of your happiness quotient.

YES NO

____ ____ I look forward to going to church on Sunday morning.

____ ____ I seldom find myself drifting off during the sermon.

____ ____ I don't look at my watch more than twice during the service

____ ____ I study my Sunday School lesson faithfully.

____ ____ I seldom criticize people at the church, including the pastor.

____ ____ I am involved in at least one outreach program of the church.

____ ____ I try very hard not to miss the meetings of my church.

____ ____ I feel my opinion is appreciated in the church.

____ ____ I refer to the church as *us* never as *them*.

____ ____ At least once a week, I tell God how much I appreciate my fellow Christians in the church.

INTERPRETING THE DATA

If you answered yes to eight or more of the ten questions in the happiness quotient, you are doing as well as any well-adjusted church member could expect. The value of this book will be primarily to firm up your faithfulness to the church. It can also give you understanding of the problems others are facing.

If you checked the yes column less than five times, you are the kind of person for whom this book is intended. Most readers fall between four and eight—not willing to give up but not receiving all the fulfillment and enjoyment from the church that they desire. If your score falls below four, you probably have left the church already.

In any case, it is not too late to get more from your church experience. The question to ask yourself is, "Once I discover a lack of fulfillment with the church, what can I do about it?"

During my own discontentment, I began by looking at each facet of the church as it related to me, searching for principles of Scripture that would give me the power to change the situation. I got this idea from Benjamin Franklin who said, "He who introduces the principles of primitive Christianity into the course of human affairs will change the face of the earth." I didn't seek to change the face of the earth. Just my own life would do.

In the following pages, you will find some of the questions I asked, as I discovered principles from the Bible which led me to chart a new course in my church. This book can't perform miracles, but it can challenge you to rethink issues. You can change if you are willing.

As you read, fill out the charts, select specific courses of action to effect conscious change, and ask the Holy Spirit to be your guide and teacher.

GUIDELINES FOR FURTHER STUDY

Lethargy. Many church members do not realize that their love for the church has grown cold until they ask questions like the ones in the happiness quotient. It's easy to become indifferent and lethargic, even when we hear sermons on renewal. Paul's advice to the church in Ephesus contained a warning for Christians. He told them, "Wake up," "Be careful how you live," "Make good use of every opportunity you have," and "Try to find what the Lord wants you to do" (Eph. 5:14-16).

As you examine your attitudes, apply the Ephesian advice by asking yourself where you have fallen asleep in your church life, how this has affected how you live, what the Lord wants you to do, and how you could be buying up opportunities to serve Him.

Image. One of the largest blocks in your way to becoming the kind of person God would have you to be is your image of yourself. It is difficult to admit that you are not all you should be. After urging us not to be conformed to the world, the Apostle Paul wrote, "Do not think of yourself more highly than you should. Instead, be modest in your thinking, and judge yourself according to the amount of faith God has given you" (Rom. 12:3).

Only as you are honest with God in assessing your feelings about yourself in relation to the church, can you hope to change them. For most Christians, the church plays an important part in helping them find the will of God for their lives. But like Elijah who heard God's voice not in the storm or the whirlwind, not in the earthquake or fire, but in a still small voice, we too hear Him when we listen with honest, quiet hearts.

Is your self-importance standing in the way of God working in your life through your church?

Attitudes. Some years ago a pastor invited a musical group to his church for an evening service. Though the church board determined to give the group an honorarium for coming, the pastor stood in the meeting and said he felt led to take a love offering. He did. The next evening the church board convened. One member reprimanded the pastor— "You said you would not take an offering, but you did. All I had was a $10 bill, and I felt obligated to contribute against my better judgment."

"I'm sure the Lord will bless you for what you did."

"Not with my attitude," said the board member.

QUESTIONS TO ASK YOURSELF

1. Am I unhappy with the way things are going in my church? If so, is that attitude affecting my relationships with other people?

2. Does it make any difference whether or not I am happy in the church, just as long as I am actively serving God?

3. As I remember back to the time when I first joined the church, in what ways has my outlook changed? For the better? For the worse?

4. The first step to solving a problem is defining it. The second step is recognizing that its solution is just around the corner.

What problems do I see that might be causing my lack of zeal in the church? What might be some of the solutions God has already prepared to get me on the right track?

CHAPTER TWO

Setting Goals
for Fulfillment

"I joined the church because it had a good youth program for our three teenagers," said a layman from Florida.

"I was a new Christian when I first joined our church," said a mother of four young children. "I didn't know anything about church doctrine, but the people were friendly and I needed that. They took an interest in me."

"I came to this church because of its good musical program. I'm not much interested in the sermons, and the church doctrine doesn't even fit my background, but I sure do like the music." So said a middle-aged man who had left another church because of the tension there.

"Truthfully," said a midwesterner who works for a Christian organization, "I came to this church because it has an early morning service. That gives me most of the day with my family."

We may talk about joining the church to serve in the body of Christ and participate in its efforts to win the world for Him. But if we are honest with ourselves, we probably have other reasons for joining the church. Some reasons may be substantial, others superficial.

If the joy is gone from your relationship with your church, it's time to ask yourself why you selected that church in the first place. If your choice was primarily for convenience, there is little surprise that the joy has departed.

Let's take a look at your reasons for joining your church. Can you remember back to that time? Since most decisions are the result of several factors rather than a single issue, check all the following which apply to you.

____ My children needed the good youth program the church provided.

____ I had friends there.

____ A family member attended there.

____ I became a believer because of someone in the church, and it was a natural thing for me to attend there.

____ I was impressed with the pastor.

____ The people were friendly.

____ It is a denomination I already belonged to.

____ I felt comfortable with the congregation.

____ It was the right size.

____ I promised someone who visited me that I would go, and I wanted to keep my promise.

____ The church had a large group of people my age.

____ It was an active church, affording many opportunities for participation.

____ The church is located near my home.

____ I liked its doctrinal position.

____ The building impressed me.

____ The church was large enough for me to get lost in the crowd so that I would not have to become involved.

____ It was the kind of church I grew up in.

____ I liked the time, length, and order of the morning service.

____ I liked the dedication to evangelism which the church had.

____ I appreciated its commitment to missions.

_____ I liked its emphasis on Christian growth.
_____ The church had a bus ministry.
_____ They had a nursery for my children.
_____ Others _____

_____   _____
_____   _____

INTERPRETING THE DATA

We may select a church on one set of criteria; if we later become unhappy there, we may judge it on quite another. That's not fair. Since we tend to blame everyone and everything but ourselves for our unhappiness, it is not uncommon to criticize the church, even if the reason for our dissatisfaction is within ourselves.

George was a Baptist layman in an oil refining town. He had been growing steadily unhappier in his church ever since he had retired from his job. He was a leader in the Awana club, a weekday activity for children, and he knew he was becoming short-tempered with them. His wife pointed out that he was disagreeable in church meetings.

When George's pastor asked me to fill the pulpit so he could get away for a needed rest, he told me, "I've arranged for you to have lunch with George. See if you can help him."

After our lunch, George took me through the place where he used to work. He told me how he had had the respect of his peers and those who worked for him. While we were there, several people asked his advice on business matters.

But when we talked about the church, George indicated that he felt a lack of respect. I admired George for his accomplishments, but I saw how he could make life miserable in the church. He was trying there to regain the leadership role he had lost by retiring from his job.

If the church is not all it should be for us, and we see frustration and anxiety setting in, the first step in recovery is to find where the problem really lies. Is it within our church or within ourselves—or both?

When you first selected your church, what expectations did you have? Does it still measure up? Is it possible that your church has fulfilled its part of the bargain? If so, you have no right to be critical of it. If your needs have changed, you might be wise to consider a move, but don't blame that on the church.

On the other hand, it may be that the church has made significant changes. It may not be the same church today that it was when you joined it. Needs that it met then it may no longer meet. Pastoral, physical, and doctrinal changes may have occurred. If so, do you look for another church, try to bring this one back to what it once was, or just make the best of it?

When Jim and Peggy came to Bethphage Chapel, they were parents of three young children. There was an active program for kids, including a preschool. Most of the church families had young children, and the median age of the membership was under thirty. People came and went through the years, until one day Peggy said, "Our children are grown and we are among the oldest members of the congregation. The church still has a preschool and still ministers primarily to a young congregation. Perhaps it's time to move on."

They still considered their church to be a good one. It had not changed, but Jim and Peggy had. Now the church was ministering to needs they no longer had. Facing retirement, they were including their church in the areas of life they needed to examine.

Age, marital status, outlook or interests may have placed you in a position similar to Jim and Peggy's, and evaluation may be in order. If so, this is a time for caution. The way you feel about your church might not be a good gauge of its ability to meet your needs. Some people have transferred ill feelings against a pastor or other members into their assessment of the church's overall ministry. Others have rejected a church because they were unhappy with a decision the leaders made. A conclusion you make while you are tired, overworked, or under stress may be the wrong one if it is not based on careful examination of the facts. As King Solomon said, "Any enterprise is built by wise planning, becomes strong through common sense, and profits wonderfully by keeping abreast of the facts" (Prov. 24:3-4, TLB).

Top-of-the-head feelings are not much on which to make a decision. The editor of a Christian magazine once received a letter from a subscriber which stated, "Your magazine is not as good at it used to be." The editor wrote back, "Madam, it never was." Since we evaluate through emotional filters , it is important to carefully screen the facts.

You already looked at the reasons you had for selecting your church. Now, imagine the church you would choose as the most ideal to meet your present needs.

____ It would have a good youth program for my children.

____ It would be a place where I already have friends.

____ It would be good if another family member attended there.

____ The church would be the one where I became a believer in Christ.

____ I would like the pastor.

____ The people would be friendly.

____ It would be of my denomination.

____ I would feel comfortable there.

____ I would go there if I promised someone I would.

____ The church would have a large group of people my age.

____ It would afford opportunities for participation.

____ It would be located near my home.

____ It would have a doctrinal position with which I agree.

____ I would be impressed with the building.

____ It would be large enough so I could choose not to be involved.

____ It would have a strong missionary emphasis.

____ It would be like the church I grew up in.
____ It would be dedicated to evangelism.
____ It would have a bus ministry.
____ It would have a nursery for my children.
____ Others _____
____   _____
____   _____
____   _____

You undoubtedly recognized most of the reasons that were in the list for joining the church initially. By comparing the two lists, does it seem that you still need the same type of church you did then?

For a change in churches to even be considered, your lists of needs and the ability of your church to fulfill those needs should be incompatible. To see if this is so, go back to the checklist you just did and underline the strong characteristics of your church.

If you underline most of the items you feel important to selecting a church, it's not likely that you will find happiness by making a change in your church membership. To obtain more fulfillment the change must be internal. On the other hand, if your needs are the same as in the first list, and the church is no longer able to meet those needs, you might consider a change.

I'm using the words *possibility* and *consider*, because it is not mandatory that your church have a strong ministry in areas where you feel the most need. Many Christians have found joy and excitement in churches by serving others; they fulfill their own needs in other ways.

However, for some, the frustration resulting from perceived needs not being met can be intense. Now is the time to make a conscious commitment to either try out some other churches or to make a definite effort to renew your vitality in your church. To stay put and follow the advice in the rest of this chapter is not an easy task, but changing churches is not easy either.

A CALL TO COMMITMENT

The church member who wants to see his relationship with the church come alive must be willing to work at it. Moving to greener pastures in another church, or dropping out altogether without first trying to resolve problems in the present situation, may be a mark of an unwillingness to take commitment seriously. When we commit ourselves to the Lord, we also commit ourselves to the Church. When we are born into God's family, we inherit the responsibility that comes with it. When we accept the Father, we accept our brothers and sisters in the faith.

The Bible says, "Let us be concerned for one another, to help one another, to show love, and to do good. Let us not give up the habit of meeting together, as some are doing" (Heb. 10:23-24). In a church as in a marriage, love can grow cold. What then?

When Bob Bennett, a thirty-eight-year-old bachelor, was ready to throw in the towel, he asked himself an important question, "What other church would better meet my needs?" Going through the same steps you did to get this far, he became convinced that his church wasn't all that bad, and decided to stay and search for ways to inject vitality into his church experience.

Bob's decision was a logical one for a believer whose love for the church has grown cold. It gave him a chance to rebuild his church life. But to do this he needed to know two things: what the church expected of him and what he could expect of the church. Bob took the direct approach, invited his pastor to lunch and shared his concern for personal revitalization.

"I suggest," said the pastor, "that each church member should have three qualities, all of which we find in Ephesians 4—6. The first is *love* among the brethren." He read Bob the first seven verses of chapter 4. "Each member must walk worthy of the vocation to which he is called," he said. "That includes being a living example of long-suffering and

29

forbearance, keeping the unity of the Spirit in the bond of peace and seeing our oneness with other Christians. A loving person respects others and seeks to promote their best interests above his own."

The pastor's second quality was *loyalty*. "Though mentioned second, this may be the most important of the three," he continued. "The church can't hold together without the loyalty of its members." He read Ephesians 5:31, " 'For this reason a man will leave his father and mother and unite with his wife and the two will become one.' There is a deep secret truth revealed in this Scripture which I understand as applying to Christ and the church."

When Bob asked what loyalty really boiled down to, the pastor listed attendance at services, involvement in the church programs, financial support, and refraining from public disagreement with church leaders. In short, Bob was to be supportive.

"Think for yourself and participate in the church decision-making process, but then support the decisions which are made," the pastor continued, "even if you disagree."

"The final point," he said, "is *labor*. Ephesians 4 tells us that Christ gave gifts to the church to prepare God's people for Christian service. It is up to me as the pastor to equip the saints for ministry. It's up to the saints to minister. That's you. Pastors feed the sheep, but the sheep reproduce other sheep. No church can be vital if the congregation waits for the pastor to be the soul-winner. We are all called to witness."

He and Bob then discussed the church's programs and the many opportunities they provided for members to be witnesses and soul-winners. "Bob," he concluded, "I'll guarantee that you will find the church to be as challenging as it was before you began to drop out, if you'll just get more involved."

It seemed to Bob that his pastor laid the success or failure for the church strictly on the shoulders of the congregation. Bob challenged this in his own mind. He knew

30

that not all pastors would do this, though the attitude might be more common than some people would like to admit. Other pastors today see themselves as servant-leaders. Their duty is to help members develop. Bob knew of pastors who wanted to see the work of the church progress and the community won to the Lord, but who placed a higher priority on the individual growth of their members than on such things as loyalty and labor.

Sometimes the difference between Bob's pastor and the servant-leader is only semantic; but it raises crucial issues of the individual and self-awareness, family relationships, community influence and personal development. Concentration on the individual may mean that the individual will not always be available to work in the church's program.

For many of us, a conversation with the pastor would be enough, but it wasn't for Bob. He went to the Bible to study the structure of the early church. In Acts 2:42-47 he found a caring community. People helped each other. Though persecuted, they were eager to learn from the Apostles and care for each other. They praised God and grew in number. Bob wondered if he could bring joy back into his church life, if he were more caring.

In Acts 20, he saw that the church was supportive. Through words of counsel, encouragement, financial aid, and prayer, they built one another up in the faith.

Bob then read through Romans and into First Corinthians where in chapter 3 he discovered that the church could never meet all his expectations because it always would be composed of imperfect people like himself. Even the godly Apollos created tension in the church. Some believers claimed to follow him while others claimed to follow Paul, all missing the point that we are to follow God.

Bob learned that the early believers continued to contribute to the cause of Christ while they worked out their differences. In the Council of Jerusalem (Acts 15) when the differences were major doctrinal issues, the believers came to Spirit-formulated and logical conclusions. They worked on their problems, rather than let their problems work on them.

That seemed to satisfy Bob. He knew that the church was God's way of caring for him, and that church was more than a place to serve God. It could be counted on to teach him more about God, and could aid him emotionally, physically, and even financially, if need be. There would be problems, but they would be worked out. Now all he needed was some way to isolate the specifics of what he wanted from the church and a way to measure his progress.

SETTING PERSONAL GOALS FOR CHURCH MEMBERSHIP

If the church is to come alive for you, there should be no question about your commitment. Long ago someone said that although the church is a leaky boat on life's sea, it is the only boat we have. We must stick with it and do what we can to make it operate effectively.

To get more from your church membership, you should first assess your needs. This is followed by setting realistic goals to meet those needs, and should include a measurable way to chart progress toward the fulfillment of the goals. Goals help direct your energies toward a specific target. They focus attention on what you wish to accomplish. Here are some tips on goalsetting:

- Build your goals on the things that concern you most.
- Keep them within your abilities.
- Believe you can accomplish them.
- Determine a way to measure your progress.
- Set target dates to act as benchmarks in reaching goals.
- Tie your goals to what you believe God wants to see happen in your church life.

Though goalsetting is work, it is also fun. And it is biblical. The Bible say, "We should make plans, counting on God to direct us" (Prov. 16:9, TLB).

We can see goalsetting in action in the life of the Apostle Paul. Because of his desire to evangelize the political leadership of Rome, and because of the Holy Spirit's call for him to preach in Jerusalem, Paul "made up his mind to travel through Macedonia and Achaia and go on to Jerusalem," on his way to Rome (Acts 19:21). In Acts 20 we read, "In obedience to the Holy Spirit I am going to Jerusalem, not knowing what will happen to me there" (v. 22).

Paul's concern, prompted by a determination to accomplish his Spirit-formulated goal, did not go unchallenged. In Caesarea when the Prophet Agabus tried to warn Paul not to go, he said, "Why are you doing this, crying like this and breaking my heart? I am ready not only to be tied up in Jerusalem but even to die there for the sake of the Lord Jesus (Acts 21:10). No goal, no matter how well-formulated, will succeed without determination to make it happen.

In this section is a chart to help you articulate your concerns, state your goals in concrete terms, and set measurable standards of accomplishment. In the concern column, record the things that bother you most about your life in the church. Some suggestions are given in the sample. For many people, concerns seem to fall into three categories: their feelings about God; their desire for Christian growth that touches the rest of life; and, finally, concern for how they relate to family members and other people who pass through their lives.

State your concerns in terms that affect you personally. For example you might say, "My concern is my lack of _____, my inability to _____, or my desire to _____."

State your goals beginning with the word *to* as in, "to understand ___," "to see change in ___," or "to feel ___." The more concrete the goal, the more effective it will be. Rather than a goal "to attend the morning service more often," say, "to attend the morning service at least ten out of the next twelve Sundays."

Relative and vague goals leave you without a way to determine if you are successful; specific goals can be measured objectively. Avoid setting unrealistic goals. Be ambitious, but don't reach beyond your ability.

Finally, state measurable standards for each goal. This tells you how you are going to go about making it work. Measurable standards help you fulfill your goals in practical situations. They are also valuable to evaluating your progress. Here is an example of how Bob went about using this thinking in setting his goals.

Immediate Concerns	Stated Goals	Measurable Standards
1. My lack of fellowship with God's people.	To get to know people.	Have three different families visit in my home over the next two months.
	To overcome my shyness in meeting people new to the services.	Introduce myself to at least one new person every other week during the first three months, but it only counts if I recall their names.
2. My desire to understand what kind of person God wants me to be.	To relate my own life to the sermons.	Buy a notebook and take notes at all the services I attend in the next three months.
	To study the Bible on my own, looking for principles related to what God expects of me.	In my notebook, I list passages which apply and record God's directives and principles. Get thirty entries in thirty days.

Setting Goals for Fulfillment

Although this is only a partial list of how Bob handled the task, it shows what can be done. Don't list more goals than you have time to accomplish; however, remember that you can often do more than you think, if you make a conscious effort. If your process seems too complex or frightens you in any way, list only the two or three concerns most important to you, with one goal and standard for each concern. A small step in the right direction is better than none.

Some people say, "I don't know where to start. I need help in locating my concerns." Here are some you might consider; they may help you define others more tailored to your needs:

- My desire to worship God in such a way that I more fully feel His presence.
- My concern for the spiritual growth of my family. (List members of the family and the concerns you have for them.)
- My desire to know more about the Bible.
- My lack of love toward someone.
- My failure to participate in church life.
- My concern that too many of my friends are from outside the church.
- My concern that I have no non-Christian friends.
- My fear of involvement in evangelism; my failure to witness.
- My desire to understand the character of God and to know why He has dealt with humanity as He has.
- My failure to encourage other Christians.
- My desire to believe that the Bible is true and can be applied to the decisions I make every day.
- My fear that I don't belong or that people don't accept me.
- My uneasiness with some action the church has taken.
- My fear of being too easily managed by other people rather than being led by the Lord.

- My determination to find God's will in a specific situation.

Once you determine your immediate concerns, it is not difficult to turn them into goals and standards. Be creative and ask yourself why you have these concerns. Remember that the church's role is, in part, to help you to become all that God wants you to be.

At this point, you may be asking yourself if all this is necessary. "When I became a Christian, I thought that God would simply change me into what He wanted me to be," you may say. "I thought that my problems would slowly fade away."

There is nothing in Scripture to indicate that the Christian life works that way. It is true that salvation is a gift of God and that it includes eternal life in His presence; but life on earth is still a struggle. Think of people like Moses, Joshua, the prophets, Paul—and even Jesus. They all had their obstacles to overcome, decisions to make, and courses to chart.

It would be nice if the church were full of mature individuals who exhibited no needs in their daily lives that weren't being fully met by the Lord. But the truth is that while we excel in one area, we may fail in another. You can probably point to people you know who have been successful in reaching people for Christ, but who have had significant tensions in their families. You have seen those who were successful as Sunday School teachers but who had continual struggles with their own spiritual lives. Some church members function well in the world, but can't seem to get it together in the church—and vice versa.

Perhaps that's why Paul referred to the church as a body. Each member helps the other. While we must guard against the attitude that the church exists only to serve us, we should not be ashamed to let it meet our needs and answer our concerns. We *can* restore lost joy to our church life if we'll make the effort.

Setting Goals for Fulfillment

Take the time necessary to complete the following chart. As you work your way through this book, return to it often and measure your progress. You may want to make a copy of the chart before filling it out. This will give you a clean chart to use in the future.

Immediate Concerns	Stated Goals	Measurable Standards

GUIDELINES FOR FURTHER STUDY

The importance of church membership. People who are unhappy with their church experience look for an alternative to the effort of being a good church member and living up to the high standards often expected. They sooner or later ask, "Should I be a member at all?" A nonmember is often not under the onus as is the member. He is free to come and go without the restraints or obligations of the member. Is this option in keeping with Hebrews 10:24? Can a person be a member of the larger universal church without being a member of the local church?

At one time I sought to attend a local church and limit my involvement by not becoming a member. The church policy allowed for nonmembers to teach Sunday School, but not to participate in the decision-making process or in administration. Soon, however, I discovered that my relationship with others in the church was hindered. Some said, "Why is he not a member? Doesn't he like us? Does he feel superior? What have we done to make him reject us?" I determined from that standpoint alone that my decision was the wrong one.

The demands of church membership. Many church members seek leisure rather than leadership. The extent of their involvement is to attend on Sundays and an occasional special service, but little else. It is almost as though their major contribution is to be another number on the church roles. They contribute financially and encourage other members with their presence. But is that enough to fulfill the obligations of membership? Does 1 Corinthians 12:19-27 imply more than this?

QUESTIONS TO ASK YOURSELF

1. If I were to make a contract with the church, what would I ask of other members and what would I agree to do for them?

Setting Goals for Fulfillment

2. Do I take my church membership seriously enough to go to the work of setting goals for myself and making my church experience meaningful?

3. Is it right for me to question what I should get from the church? Does this violate the trust relationship I have with the church?

4. Have I let petty disagreements and relatively unimportant matters keep me from fellowship and enjoyment in the church? How can I solve this problem?

CHAPTER THREE

Taking Advantage of Opportunities

Because Bill and Sue were unhappy with the little church they were attending, a colleague in Bill's office encouraged them to visit a large, well-known church across town. They drove the five miles to the church and after parking the car at the direction of a parking attendant, they were ushered through massive doors toward the narthex where they were to meet Bill's friend. "I can't believe the size of this place!" Bill told Sue, as they waited.

"Good morning, Bill," came a voice from across the narthex. In a moment, Bill's colleague was there welcoming the couple. They felt better now that someone was there to guide them.

Many things seemed new and strange to Bill and Sue. The pastor wore a robe and addressed God on behalf of the congregation. Unfamiliar symbols adorned the walls, and some of the hymns were new to them. Though it was not what they were used to, they liked the service and felt they had a common bond with other believers.

Across town that morning was another couple, Marge and Ralph. They were members of the large church which Bill and Sue were visiting, but they had decided to attend a smaller church this Sunday. They knew no one there but had driven by the church several times and always thought they would like to visit. Although they had not verbalized it to each other, they were looking for a church that would allow them to slow down and, in a sense, retreat from the hectic role they had grown into in their church. At one time Ralph had been a trustee, and now he was a deacon. They attended most of the meetings for people their age, but now they were getting older and thought that reduced involvement would allow them to get closer to the Lord and to each other.

They entered the wood-stained doors into a hallway which led to the sanctuary. They hung their coats on the metal rack and walked into the sanctuary. Just inside the door, an usher smiled and gave them a bulletin with a scenic view on the cover and the mimeographed order of service inside. The bulletin seemed more homey than what they were used to in their large church. They remarked about how it was written more personally as if everyone knew each other.

The sermon wasn't as polished as what they would have heard in their church, but the pastor was sincere and displayed a good background in the Scripture. Some of the songs they sang that morning they had not heard since they were teenagers. The singing brought back memories of happy times and they remarked about an old Ford they used to drive to church when they were first married. "I think I'm going to like this," said Marge.

IN SEARCH OF MEANING

What do Bill and Sue and Marge and Ralph have in common other than all being visitors to new churches and finding a feeling of fellowship and acceptance? Both couples are making conscious efforts to replace their church experiences with others they hope will bring the joy they once knew.

Like many people in search of a more meaningful church

life, they are entertaining rather drastic measures to solve their problems. They are willing to leave long-standing friends and commitments to rekindle the feelings they once had. They may yet go to other churches before they find one that is right for them.

These couples are in a critical time, because the decisions they make will change their lives significantly. Church is important to them and they want it to be right.

Casual visits can tell you a lot about a church. You see how members treat one another and watch social and relational aspects of church life that may indicate how well you will fit in. Sermons are bound to express the theological emphases of the church.

Perhaps if Bill and Sue, Ralph and Marge had taken the time to examine their concerns and build programs to revitalize their experiences in their own churches, they would never have wanted to visit other churches.

It is unfortunate that so often we are swayed by our feelings rather than the facts. When I was pastoring a church in Indiana some years ago, a woman's husband died, necessitating her move from a large city to our rural area. For several weeks she attended my church; she liked the people, perhaps because they liked her.

One day she said to me, "Pastor, I want to move my membership here because you and my former pastor are so much alike and believe the same things. I know I'll be happy here."

It was hard for me to believe that her pastor and I believed the same things. I was a fundamentalist, he quite liberal. Our ideas and theology were far apart; but for the woman seeking membership, that didn't matter. We were both friendly and we both referred to the Bible when we delivered our sermons. Her profession of faith seemed genuine, and she joined the church and was a faithful member for my tenure there. I appreciated the opportunity to teach the Bible to her and to influence her theology. However, when I see someone joining a church, I still think of her and wonder how many people make major decisions on feelings rather than facts.

Bruce Shelley, professor of church history at the Conservative Baptist Theological Seminary in Denver, Colorado, says, "The run-of-the-mill American, Joe Average, does not go to church out of denominational loyalty or out of doctrinal convictions. He may go the first time out of a host of reasons, but he will go back only if the church is winsome and caring."[1]

Once a move is made, the people seldom return to their original church. They often feel the leaving was an act of rejection and they would rather not open those wounds.

Bob Bennett, whom we met in Chapter 2, was one who examined the facts concerning his life and his church. He articulated his concerns and set goals. He was going to find fulfillment in his church membership. Then he did something unexpected—he took a long hard look at four basic areas in the church which were to form a bridge between his goals and his involvement in the church program. His thinking was due in part to something his pastor had said— "I'll guarantee that you'll find the church to be as exciting as it was before you began to drop out if you'll just get more involved." Bob knew that he wanted to be involved, but not just for the sake of involvement. He had a lot of things going on, and his time was limited. At this point, his part in the church program was more for his benefit than for the church. So he systematically looked at how the church could minister to him while he was serving in its program.

THE WORSHIP SERVICES

Bob knew that worship was vital to establishing a personal relationship to God. Worship provides teaching, fellowship and an opportunity to reverence God. He needed that.

He thought that if he were in a liturgical church, he would feel closer to God in worship. It seemed there would be more opportunity for congregational participation; the sermons were shorter and the mood more quiet. The sermon was a focal point and often was instructional rather than an effort to engender a feeling of the presence of God and an awe of His greatness. But he wondered if he would feel at home with a more formal service.

Most people seem to feel at home in an atmosphere consistent with their background and the kind of church they attended when they were young. Though not true in every case, it seems to be the educational and economic heritage more than the formality or informality that determines how comfortable we are.

Usually it is difficult to transfer from one form of worship to another. Even changes in our traditional patterns can be traumatic. When the Catholic church began to say mass in English rather than Latin, some Catholic friends remarked to me about how uncomfortable they felt.

Rev. Clio Thomas, pastor of the Advent Christian Church in Seattle and adjunct professor at Fuller Theological Seminary, wrote in the *Advent Christian Witness*,

> Worship is getting outside ourselves and getting lost in the transcendence of God. Any Sunday, for example, that we go to church saying, "I hope I'll get something today," the chances are we won't get anything. We started on the wrong foot. We must go to worship saying, "What can I bring to God? What can I offer Him, from my life, my being, my person, my thinking, from my mind?"[2]

Bob knew that if the church were to assist him in meeting goals related to the worship of God, the morning service would be a key part of that process. So he set up four questions on which to judge how well the church could minister to him through the morning worship experience.

YES NO
___ ___ Are the services God-centered, rather than primarily instructional and congregational in nature?

Taking Advantage of Opportunities

___ ___ Am I a participant in the worship more than I am a spectator?

___ ___ Does the average service influence my view of the character of God and affirm my faith in Him?

___ ___ Do I feel closer to God as a result of my worship experience?

You can rate your worship experiences along with Bob. Considering the last three services you attended, give yourself one point for each yes answer. Remember the number, as you will use it later.

TEACHING MINISTRIES

Bob Bennett determined that if his attitude were right, and if he were adequately prepared, his church would be a valuable place in which to worship God; but worship was not the only thing that concerned him. Could he learn enough from the other church ministries to satisfy his need for biblical knowledge—one of his written concerns?

Teaching ministries are vital to personal growth. Instruction in the Bible and application of its truths become the foundation on which we build our lives and find much of our satisfaction. Bob knew that if the church did not have adequate opportunities for him to learn, it would be hard for him to reach the goals he had set to improve his understanding of the Bible. He began to examine his church's program of teaching.

Though Bob's church had not caught the vision of systematically teaching through the Bible to give a complete Bible education to the congregation over a period of years, it realized the importance of a well-developed program. It seemed to have something for almost everyone. And if he could not find what he wanted in the church, he could take advantage of the Bible studies in his area.

In a sense, the sermons were heavily into teaching. The pastor taught in both the morning and evening services. Usually he would take a book of the Bible and explain it

45

verse by verse in the expository tradition. Several organizations are currently trying to encourage more pastors to concentrate on this method of sermon development. Two of these are Stephen Olford's Institute for Biblical Preaching and the Committee on Biblical Preaching.

Bob's church encouraged its people in study of the Bible by placing notepads in the hymnal racks, for taking notes on the sermons.

Bob listed four more questions to rate his church on how likely the church was to teach him what he needed to fulfill his goals.

YES NO
___ ___ Does a Sunday School class for my age systematically teach the Bible?
___ ___ Can I recall three ideas from the last sermon I listened to?

_____
_____
_____

___ ___ Does the church provide other learning situations such as home Bible studies, conferences, and seminars?
___ ___ Has my knowledge of the Bible grown significantly in the past year?

As you check your church by this list, give yourself one point for each yes answer (only one point for question 2). Add this number to the score of the worship service questions.

EVANGELISTIC OUTREACH

Many churches regard missionary activity to be their primary evangelistic outreach. North America sends out more missionaries than any other part of the world. Today missions is a growing concern and a big business—the budgets of mission organizations are constantly increasing; most mailing lists are on computer; missions pay for consultants to write appeal letters and plan fundraising.

Yet most people in the church have very little concept of just how much their church is involved in preaching the Gospel around the world. Bob knew the name of only one of the missionaries his church supported.

But for Bob, it was not the missionary program which would help him fulfill his personal concerns and goals for outreach. Being a shy person, he was aware of his need to relate to non-Christians and to share his faith. So Bob looked to the program of the church to see if there might be a way to gain experience and confidence in witnessing. His church ran the usual ministries for youth—Vacation Bible School, weekday activity clubs, Sunday School, and occasionally a parent-child outing. Perhaps he could gain experience there. But Bob didn't feel all that comfortable being with kids. Was there any other avenue open to him?

His church did not have a program for single people and the college group was pretty well closed to all but a few people who had worked with it for the past several years. He could go out on his own and pray that God would bring people across his path with whom he could share his faith; but without help this was not likely to happen.

He thought of other organizations, those outside the church, which might provide such a platform. Some people in his town ran a rescue mission. Someone else gathered up old clothes, furniture, and appliances for refugees and people going through hard times. There were organizations working on the community college campus, a major ethnic group ministry and . . . . The more he thought, the more possibilities opened to him.

What bothered him was whether his church would approve of this outside involvement, and whether it would help or hinder his attempt to accomplish his outreach goals.

Evangelism outreach that is conducted apart from the church can have drawbacks as well as rewards. Some pastors and church leaders feel threatened by their people ministering outside the church. Bob's pastor tended this way—he didn't like to see Bob's energy spent outside when the church had so much to do. "The place that's ministering to you needs to be the place where you minister," said his pastor.

As he considered this, Bob made his third checklist.

YES NO

____ ____ Does my church provide at least one outreach program that could help me reach evangelism-related goals?

____ ____ Can I name three missionaries my church supports?

_____

_____

_____

____ ____ Has my church taught me how to share my faith? Are the people of my church models to help me in evangelism?

As you rate your church add another point for each yes, (only one point on question 2).

SOCIAL PROGRAMS AND ENTERTAINMENT

We have looked at worship, teaching, and outreach; but if we are honest with ourselves, most of our concerns surface in the social life of the church. Many people are members of churches which have weak worship services, poor teaching ministries, and little outreach; yet these people are happy because their social needs are being met.

Many people today look at the church as a family. They want services that are less formal and allow time for sharing concerns and blessings as well as items for prayer. Such meetings build a family feeling and kinship.

The family warmth in the church has brought more people to Christ and into the church than all outreach programs combined. And this reminds us of Jesus's words, "If you have love for one another, then everyone will know that you are My disciples" (John 13:35). Many people have joined a church because they have seen its members showing love. When churches experience tension, they seldom grow in numbers or see many conversions. While this is partly due to the channeling of energies to the area of tension, it is also due to a lack of the expression of their love for others.

Bob realized the critical link to meeting many of his concerns was involvement in the social life of the church. He needed the counsel and encouragement of other Christians, and he needed to feel needed. No amount of involvement in the program of the church could supplant his need for fellowship.

The Sunday School class for his age was his most obvious social group. People who come to Sunday worship and avoid Sunday School or its appropriate counterpart will surely feel they are on the outside looking in.

Bob found that the Sunday School class was only the beginning. There were other groups such as the choir, informal settings at concerts, and evangelistic functions. At first Bob looked on some of the social settings as entertainment, but he soon found that they can build valuable links of understanding and commitment between those who take advantage of them. Bob added some of these events to his list of measurable standards which were to be the outworking of his goals. Here is Bob's final checklist.

YES NO

____ ____ Have I been invited to attend one social gathering in the past month?

____ ____ Do I feel that the small groups in the church would accept me if I attended them?

____ ____ I feel closer to the people of the church after attending a social function.

____ ____ What three good things does the church do for me that my family did for me when I was growing up?

_____

_____

_____

The Library
INTERNATIONAL CHRISTIAN
GRADUATE UNIVERSITY

Again, give yourself one point for each yes (one point for question 4).

SUMMARIZING YOUR FINDINGS

Total each of the yes answers on the four checklists. Of the total of sixteen, if you had twelve or above, your church is offering you a balanced approach to help you meet your concerns and goals. Either you are already happy with your church experience, or are simply not taking advantage of a good thing.

A total of eight to twelve may indicate you are on rather shaky ground. It's going to require extra effort to see your church minister to you in achieving your goals, but you can make it if you exert the effort. You might have to take the initiative to break into social groups or introduce new evangelism ministries to the church.

Fewer than eight yes answers means that you cannot expect much help from the church in building new attitudes toward it and its role in your life. You may find that to make things work there, you will have to seek involvement in parachurch or outside ministries. Make it a priority to get to know the pastor and leaders of the church. Find the social groups that are for your age and make friends. Invite people over for coffee, tea, or pizza.

When Bob Bennett added up his score, he felt pleased about his church. It was almost as though he was already on his way to bring a new attitude to his church experience. He could see the climate changing and he was growing excited about what lay in store.

GUIDELINES FOR FURTHER STUDY

The purpose of the church. Some people challenge the idea that the church has any personal responsibility for its members. They claim that the church is called of God to do His will and should spend its time in service, namely evan-

50

gelism. The individual church member must defer to the guidance of the church elders.

In one church, a young man was told by his elders that he should not marry the girl in whom he was interested. They felt such a union would take away his efforts from the Lord's service. He complied and broke off the relationship, not wishing his own interests to stand in the way of serving the Lord.

In another church, members are encouraged to make their own decisions. Lay people hear sermons on self-awareness, assertiveness, and the belief that there is nothing the believer can't do because God is personally leading him. Stressing Philippians 4:19, "And with all his abundant wealth through Christ Jesus, my God will supply all your needs," and the doctrine of the priesthood of the believer, they refrain from making decisions for him.

Jesus gave up His own interests for the interests of others. He taught when He was tired. He kept on healing, even though He was criticized. He laid down His life for all.

Yet Jesus also showed compassion on the crowds. He cried over the city of Jerusalem and treated Judas, His betrayer, with respect and dignity. In the synagogue, Jesus said, "The Spirit of the Lord is upon Me, because He has chosen Me to bring good news to the poor. He has sent Me to proclaim liberty to the captives and recovery of sight to the blind, to set free the oppressed and announce that the time has come when the Lord will save His people" (Luke 4:18-19). By word and action, Jesus showed that He wanted to help people become all they were capable of being.

As we apply His concern to our lives, we need to strike a balance between expecting the church to build us up, and working to build the church.

QUESTIONS TO ASK YOURSELF

1. Can I be a mature Christian without concentrating on making it happen through my own efforts?

2. Should I remain in a church situation that doesn't minister to me, for the sake of serving others?

3. Do I take advantage of programs my church offers to help me grow and reach my goals?

4. What is the role of parachurch ministries in helping me meet my goals?

CHAPTER FOUR

Determining Your Level of Involvement

Ron, a clean-cut family man of about thirty-five, stood openmouthed in the foyer of the church. He couldn't believe what he was hearing. Barbara Jurgens, a perky Sunday School superintendent, held his arm, urging him to accept a teaching position with the fifth grade boys' class. Her husband, Jeremiah Jurgens, was holding his other arm, asking him to commit himself to the weekly visitation program with a view to becoming its chairman in six months or so.

"When we heard you had become a member of our church, it became a contest to see which one of us would get to you first," said Barbara.

To their chagrin, they were both too late. One of the deacons who was in the meeting where Ron and his family were interviewed for membership had "scooped" the Jurgens and signed up Ron to help with Awana, the weekday activity club.

Because he had been extremely frustrated and overworked in a former church, Ron had been attending here for nearly two years as a nonmember. But now that he was part of the church, there were more jobs crying for his attention than he could possibly fill. The way the needs of the church were presented to him, it seemed he was their only hope. How could the church possibly get along without him? How had they managed before he became a member?

Although not all churches send recruiters like vultures on fresh prey, Ron's experience is not that foreign to many. "We ask new people to become involved in the church because the church needs them and they need to be working," say many pastors. "Active churches need many people to keep programs rolling, the saints growing, and new people coming to Christ."

Few people would question these reasons for wanting church members to take an active part. The personnel needs for operating a church can be immense. There are Sunday School classes to teach, activity programs to direct, meetings to plan, countless committees, and the music program. Just think of the people who serve behind the scenes: parking attendants, audio and video controllers, ushers, fellowship meal planners, library attendants, coffee servers . . . . The list seems endless. And the church need not be large either. Some churches feel they are not doing the job unless everyone has an office.

EXCUSES FOR NOT SERVING

As any person who has served on a church nominating committee can tell you, getting people to accept a church job is not all that easy. Hence the reason for the hype.

The excuses people give for refusing have not appreciably changed over the years. Some say, "I'm not a speaker and I'm in good company, for Moses had the same problem." Others say, "I can't serve because I've never been to Bible school." When Gideon was appointed by the Lord to rescue Israel from the Midianites, he said, "But Lord, how can I rescue Israel? My clan is the weakest in the tribe of Manasseh, and I am the least important member of my family" (Jud. 6:15-16). Perhaps the excuse given most often is, "I'm just too busy." That reminds us of the replies to the invitation to the great feast in Jesus' parable in Luke 14. The people all had more important things to do than dining with the master.

Some people truly don't see the need for service in the church. "Let those serve who want to, but I see it as a waste of time." At one time in my early pastoral career, I served a church that reopened after being vacant for several years. I was calling in the community and asked one man to come to church on Sunday. "I would come," he said, "if I knew that the church had enough people to remain open." He didn't come and several others followed his example, waiting to see if there would be enough people to keep it going. Soon the church was empty again and the grass grew tall about the windows.

Many excuses proceed from legitimate fears and concerns. When parishioners hesitate to accept responsibility, it may, in some cases, be that their church is asking them to perform jobs which don't seem necessary or important. Churches have long been accused of "committeeing" their people to death. If a church seeks to actively employ its members, the service must be meaningful so they can see their talents being used. A person lost in a large committee may feel that he is contributing too little—certainly not to the saving of souls or the alleviation of suffering.

Whether you are new to a church, or have just gone through the process of working out goals to renew your vitality in the church, you may be apprehensive about getting involved. Even if you know you need to serve to bring about important changes in your life, it may be hard for you to accept a job without mouthing an excuse. Take courage from the account of Ananias, in Acts 9:10-18. He was afraid to seek out Saul of Tarsus, even when told to do so by God. He knew about Saul's reputation and the potential danger to himself. It took strength to obey God and rely on His protection. And if Ananias had not obeyed and gone to Saul, the early church might never have developed as it did. In a similar way, had not missionaries, pastors and Christian workers throughout the years obeyed God's call, many of us might not have had an opportunity to hear the Gospel. Don't let fears become excuses. If God calls you to serve, respond to Him in obedience.

EFFECTS OF OVERCOMMITMENT

Some people are so involved in the church that they neglect family and vocational responsibilities.

A deacon in a small suburban church arrived home late from a church board meeting. His wife formally introduced him to his teenage son saying, "This is your father. He is gone so many nights and so much on weekends that I want you to treasure this memory until you meet again in heaven." Unfortunately, in telling the story, this man was boasting of his service to the church; he should have been taking the incident to heart.

People have been known to take on excessive church involvement because they are fleeing from problems at home. The church offers them a sanctuary where they can lose themselves in service and ignore the difficulties of daily life.

Overcommitment, especially when coupled with insensitivity, can be devastating to family members. Stories abound of Christian leaders who have been so busy in the Lord's work that their children have suffered.

A church leader in the Midwest once told me he could not understand why his teenage son had rejected his values when he had done all he could to bring him up in the nurture and admonition of the Lord. He was proud of the example of dedication he had set. "My office was in my home," he said, "and many nights I would counsel with distraught and angry church members or pastors of churches filled with tension." Because the son's room was directly above the study, I assume he heard many of those conversations. I wonder how much he was influenced by what he heard to reject his father's faith.

When you consider church involvement, you also must

consider your needs and the needs of family members. With few exceptions, everyone should be serving in some way; but parents with young children or children with special needs have God-given responsibilities that no one else may be able to carry. In 1 Timothy 3:4, Paul says a church leader is to "manage his own family well and make his children obey him with all respect." In large measure, teaching your children to obey with all respect must be done during their formative years. Time spent with your children when they are young may benefit the cause of Christ in their later years; but a child neglected in favor of the parent's service may result in a teenager who chooses not to follow Christ, and in the diminished effectiveness of the parent as well.

But parents should not rule out church involvement. Sometimes their children can be in the groups where their parents minister. When my children were young, I led a Christian Service Brigade program in the church. My son, now an adult who spends his summers at Brigade camp, looked forward to being at meetings with me, and I was able to help other boys as well.

YOUR LEVEL OF INVOLVEMENT

Sometimes our lives are ripe for service, while at other times they are not. The Apostle Paul urged unmarried people to stay single; service for God was his reason. "An unmarried man concerns himself with the Lord's work, because he is trying to please the Lord. But a married man concerns himself with worldly matters, because he wants to please his wife; and so he is pulled in two directions"(1 Cor. 7:32-34). Though the church today lacks the urgency of the early church, the principle remains—there is a time to concentrate on service at the expense of other interests, and that time varies with each person.

For many, a suitable time for taking on major commitments to the church is when they become empty nesters. Because of experience, maturity, and availability, they are in demand as workers in God's vineyard. Unfortunately, some older people take on church service, looking for the ego enhancement they lost when they retired from vocational pursuits. It's one thing to look for something meaningful to do, and quite another to promote one's own importance.

If you have articulated your concerns, set your goals, and looked at what the church has to offer in the way of programs to help you stimulate an otherwise sagging Christian experience, you need to determine just how much your particular situation can allow you to become involved in the ministry of the church.

It is wise to examine your availability and interests before you are faced with the many invitations to work. The place to start is in reexamining your commitment. You are concerned that you get from your church membership all that you feel God would want you to have. However, this concern does not necessarily mean that you will commit yourself to the hard work that makes it happen.

Ideally you are always in fellowship with the Lord; but realistically your Christian life ebbs and flows. If this were not so, Paul would have had no need to advise Timothy, "Be consistent, when it is convenient and when it is not convenient" (2 Tim. 4:2). Is your life with the Lord strong enough to cause you to hang in there when the going gets tough? Can you say in the words of the song, "If no one joins me, still I will follow"? If you accept a job without commitment to the ministry of Jesus Christ, or if you accept it only as a means to meet your goals for yourself, your interest may wear thin in a short time. One Sunday School teacher in a church I pastored told me, "If they don't appreciate my teaching, I'm through." If we are serving ourselves only and not committed to what our service will accomplish in the lives of others, there is little chance we'll stick with it.

That doesn't mean that you hold off serving the Lord until your house is all in order and you are a model church member. Few of us would ever teach or preach, or even park cars, for that matter, if that were necessary. Remember the Prophet Jonah? Yet, when he repented, Nineveh also had the opportunity to repent and turn to God. Even in times of spiritually low ebb, people have been used by God to accomplish great things.

You should not look only at your motivation for service but also consider your available time. Given your family responsibilities, time spent earning a living, sleeping, exercising, and in recreation, determine how much flexible time you can commit to the ministries of the church. Before you say, "I have absolutely no time available," consider how that could be redirected to church involvement.

But a need to serve and available time are not enough for successful service. According to 1 Corinthians 12, God has given gifts to the members of the church with which to serve Him. What you enjoy doing is often linked to the gifts God has given you. Perhaps it is because you have cultivated those skills or that people have recognized these traits in you and encouraged you. When you do something well, you like doing it. Positive attitudes, enforced by positive experiences, grow as you do.

For example, when a young father came to Christ, I wanted him to gain a closer attachment to the church and to have the opportunity to develop as a Christian. He had interest in the out-of-doors, but we needed a treasurer. Yet, when I was told that he had personal financial problems, I ruled out the treasurer's job and asked him to help with the boys club.

What do you do well? What ministry outreach would you like to develop? Your interests and abilities are the glasses through which you look at prospective ministries. If you accept responsibility in an area for which you do not have the appropriate gifts, and if you fail, the negative experience will make it hard to serve the Lord in the future.

Don't wait till you have been asked to serve, even though that seems to be the accepted way in some churches. Volunteering allows you to pick from several jobs, as opposed to accepting or rejecting each job as it comes up.

Though every member has an obligation to the local church, not all activity must be centered there. There are times when your church experience will be better if your service is outside the church. The ministry may benefit as well. Remember the Studebaker? My younger son and I belong to a group of people who own these precious jewels. Once a month we meet to discuss our hobby. Some people there may not have access to the Gospel if I drop those relationships in favor of attending another church service or serving on another committee. The same could be said of a little league baseball team, a one-to-one friendship, or a political or civic opportunity. What some call secular commitments can be God's opportunities to represent Him. They can also be excuses to keep us from serving in the church.

Some forms of service are corporate in that they take several people working together to accomplish the ministry. Other service generates through a single individual. A friend of mine began to work with four high school boys at the local YMCA. He interested them in a Bible study, and each Tuesday for several months met with them at 6 A.M. A mature couple went from door-to-door calling on their neighbors and formed a Bible study which lasted over a year.

The options are limitless when your priorities are established. Perhaps understanding how you should serve Christ could be compared to the way a radio selects the signal you hear. The air itself is flooded with stations. If your receiver amplified them all at once, your ears would be flayed with noise. The receiver screens out all the signals except the one it is tuned to, and amplifies that one alone. Likewise, most Christians can do many jobs in the church, but they will be most efficient if they select one or two and give those their best efforts. Then they will serve with order and harmony.

Determining Your Level of Involvement

PERSONAL INVOLVEMENT PROFILE

The following chart is designed to help you focus your service into the areas where you can do the most good. The discipline of listing your interests and gifts should help you understand yourself better. Defining your available time may help you to conclude that you are not as busy as you've been telling yourself. On the other hand, it may show you that you can't afford to add any more jobs unless you free yourself from some present responsibility. It is better to do a few things well and be happy, than to attempt too much and feel frustrated.

Remember that your level of service is not synonymous with your spirituality. Many people who are dedicated to Christ and His cause do not hold many jobs in the church. And conversely, it is possible for very involved people to lack Christian character, ethics, and compassion. Some of the lowest times for me spiritually were when I was most involved in the church. I experienced the barrenness of a busy life.

You may not be able to complete all the categories on the chart until you do some research into the programs and needs of your church. Using the model, list your interests as they occur to you. Do the same with your gifts, and your time, and opportunities for service. Tie together the items that relate to each other, as in the example.

Interests	Gifts	Available Time	Opportunities
auto repair	knowledge of the Bible	evenings, 7-10	neighborhood Bible study
reading	good voice	Saturday, 10-4	public relations
talking	success at soul-winning	Sunday School hour	Awana club leader
teaching	good at counseling	mornings, until 7:30	deacon
football	good cook	———	Jr. high boys' Sunday School

61

Obviously, you are going to be most happy doing both what you like to do and what you do well. If your time is not overcommitted, and the church has needs that relate to your goals, the match is a natural one. Begin with this thinking and you are on your way to a realistic level of involvement that will contribute greater fulfillment from your church experience.

HOW TO SAY NO AND MEAN IT

Educator Thomas Dewey is credited with saying, "A problem well defined is half solved." That applies to service in the church. Once you have determined where your abilities can be best used, you are better able to know what you should do. You'll find it helpful to modify your involvement profile from year to year and to be sure it complements the activities of other family members.

Your involvement profile allows you to be selective in service. You can say no and mean it, if the job offered does not fit into your profile. You can say with confidence, "I think that is an important function, but it is not one of my interests or my gifts. So although I have time to do it, I'll pass and wait for something that better fits me." No need to feel guilty, or to say yes and do a poor job.

Your satisfaction with the church depends in a measure on your level of involvement; so if you are looking for something to do, don't take a job for which you are unsuited. One will come along where you will fit. God has much to be done and intends to use all His people who are willing. Parachurch ministries such as Youth for Christ, rescue ministries, and Christian supporting organizations may provide you opportunities, if your church does not.

On the other hand, if you say no too often, someone may challenge your sincerity. Remember that the Holy Spirit gives gifts for the good of the church (1 Cor. 12:7), and it is the Spirit's responsibility to bring together the people to accomplish His purposes. This may mean that churches should not try to offer all the programs they have in the past. They might do better to concentrate on creative programs that meet needs in the membership and the community.

GUIDELINES FOR FURTHER STUDY

The urgency of evangelism. Can the church today afford to cut back on its programs? If the return of Christ is near, should we not sacrifice family, possessions, and all our own interests to witness for Him? In Luke 12:31, Jesus promised that God would meet the needs of His followers. Can we afford to refuse any job in the church in the light of this promise?

On the other hand, Paul reminded Timothy, "If anyone does not take care of his relatives, especially the members of his own family, he has denied the faith and is worse than an unbeliever" (1 Tim. 5:8). Are these passages in conflict? Can we satisfy both claims, or are we spiritually lacking when we block out time for family, friendships, and personal recreation at the expense of participating in the church program? It is difficult for the church to live under persecution; it is also difficult when it lives under affluence.

Membership implies responsibility. In 1 Corinthians 12:12-26, Paul tells us that we are all members of one body and accountable to each other. Does this imply that we should take on as much responsibility as we can? Are we being irresponsible if we refuse some jobs and require those we do accept to fit into our involvement profile?

If we refuse to participate in an area where help is needed, someone who is already overworked may assume that task. What is our responsibility to the burdened worker?

The role of the Holy Spirit. There are many instances in the Bible when God did not sanction the plans of men. He had other ideas, as with Gideon (Jud. 6) and Moses (Ex. 4). Conversely, you may decide to refuse an opportunity that the Spirit of God would want you to take. How can you be flexible enough to allow the Holy Spirit to override your logic?

QUESTIONS TO ASK YOURSELF

1. Am I willing to serve God in whatever He should ask, without reservation and at any cost?

2. Am I involved in my church to the proper level? Should I increase or decrease that involvement?

3. Have I let nonessentials take the place of Christian service for me? Should some of these be set aside so I can be more effective for the cause of Christ?

4. Am I already so committed to the cause of Christian service that relationships with my family are suffering?

5. What is the first decision I must make toward seeking positive changes in my level of involvement, and what will be the outcome if I make those changes?

CHAPTER FIVE

Preparing to Worship

We've all sat through church services where the sermons seem to be reruns, the music drags, and the prayers sound more like eloquent verbiage than soul-rending contrition. And we privately admit to endless mind-wanderings—things we have to do around the house or the enjoyment of being with a special friend.

Perhaps it is the hassle of getting ready for church that keeps you from concentrating during the service—kids, clothes, breakfast, traffic—by the time you get there, you are in no mood to worship.

On the other hand, the service itself may be so predictable that it has lost its excitement. The mere repetition of the service format, themes centering on the familiar that leave obscure Scripture passages still obscure, the same illustrations cropping up again and again, and singing from hymnbooks which automatically fall open to the same hymns—all of this puts the morning worship experience in danger of becoming commonplace.

Yet, even though the services may be lacking, we continue to show up Sunday after Sunday. Why?

One answer may lie in the acceptance we receive from other Christians and the way they support us in living out our daily lives. Other church members help us know the mind of God and determine if we are meeting His expectations for us. We still believe that the church has our best interests at heart and seeks to help us become all that we are capable of becoming.

I remember attending a worship service where my major impression was the acceptance and support of the Christians who attended. The service was led by the Romanian Missionary Society and one of the sermons was in Romanian, since many of the people attending spoke no English. I didn't understand what the speaker was saying, but I felt an acceptance and knew that together we were praising God. Just being together in the body of Christ has its rewards.

But most of us look to the church service to prepare us to face the problems and opportunities of the week ahead. In his book, *Company of the Committed*, Elton Trueblood referred to the church building as "primarily designed as a drill hall for the Christian task force." He said, "What happens on Sunday is defensible only as preparation for the daily ministry of the week which follows."[1]

The Apostle Peter advised, "Be ready at all times to answer anyone who asks you to explain the hope you have in you" (1 Peter 3:15). To fulfill our need to have answers to the problems that face us in our society, more churches are going to have to reevaluate their tendency to stay away from controversial issues.

If the church provides only fellowship and fails to give information and motivation for believers to carry back into their lives, it can't expect to hold them for long. Church meetings must be both interesting *and* substantive or people are likely to get bored and drop out.

WHAT CHURCHES ARE DOING TO REVERSE THE TREND

"We know that a vital church program is one of the things that keeps people coming," says one midwestern pastor.

"We're doing everything we can to keep from failing them there."

Programs include elective Sunday School classes, mid-week teaching, entertaining musical programs, religious celebrities, seminars, workshops, and conferences. Even drive-in services have been tried with varying amounts of success. Church leaders today are hoping that these programs will do more than attract. They hope the programs will meet basic congregational needs.

And how are they discovering what the needs of the congregation are? Often elaborate and sophisticated surveys have been used to isolate attitudes, interests, and opinions. For example, one church surveyed its congregation and felt the answer to apathy lay in the fact that people didn't know one another. The church became sensitive to the issue and launched a program to build the church family.

But trying to satisfy felt needs is not the only reason people attend church. Many go out of loyalty to God. It's a way of saying to the world, "I believe in God, the church, and the truth of the Bible." Christians turn out Sunday after Sunday to tell the world that our cause is good. "We come, not for what we can get from it but to demonstrate our loyalty to God," said one parishioner.

CHURCH STRUCTURE CONTRIBUTES TO WORSHIP

Churches seem to specialize in one of three areas. Though there is much overlap and many differences in individual congregations, churches tend to stress motivation, confession, or opportunity for self-expression. Usually you will feel more comfortable in one type of church than the others. Your reasons are cultural, as well as theological. You cannot automatically assume that your church is more pleasing to God just because you feel more at home there.

In Pentecostal worship, for example, self-expression is encouraged. Raymond Crowley, assistant general overseer of the Church of God says, "Hand-clapping and time-keeping by the patting of the feet have always been a part of our worship. In some churches, however, these expressions have been eliminated. Churches that are known as worshiping churches are providing methods whereby every person in attendance can express himself in praise to God."[2]

Worship through jubilation has become the earmark of the Church of God because it ministers to the worship needs of people who feel comfortable with it. Ray H. Hughes, president of Lee College, a Church of God school in Cleveland, Tennessee, says, "Pentecostal preachers preach for a response; and as part of worship, Pentecostal people respond. Therefore, many Pentecostal worship services conclude with the participation of the congregation in praise, prayer, and worship together."[3]

Many denominations place a greater value on the motivational aspect of the service than on self-expression or confession. It has been suggested that denominations such as Baptists and Methodists have moved the tent meeting indoors. The hymns and prayers center attention on God, but the sermon brings the service into focus and elicits the response. After an especially powerful sermon on Christian living delivered at a Bible church, one parishioner said of the pastor, "He sure parted our hair in the right place. We needed that."

Lum and Abner of 1940s radio fame demonstrate that tradition in a conversation between Abner and Grandpappy.

"Brother Parish, he preached. We all set out in the yard and he preached all afternoon. One of the best out-loud talkers I believe I ever set under."

"Yeah," said Abner. "I heard him preach. When he gets to talking about vice, 'workings of old Satan' as he calls it, he'll cut the dirt right out from under your feet."

"Oh, yeah," replied Grandpappy. "He had us all setting around there the other afternoon squirming like we was a being pestered by a wasp."[4]

Some church members can't feel they have had a worship experience unless a significant amount of time has been spent in confessing sin, expressing contrition, and praying for a reestablishing of broken fellowship with God. We often think of this when we think of Catholic worship, but the same holds true for churches in the Lutheran and Episcopal traditions.

What we need at any point in our personal lives, what we feel toward God, and the strength of our relationship with Him and His Son, Jesus Christ, have a strong influence on how we are able to worship.

Our worship patterns reveal much about how we perceive God. Even group worship is one of the most personal things we do. "Corporate worship," says the Church of God's general director of youth and Christian education, R. Lamar Vest, "was never intended to generate enough movement to take people to the throne of God when they don't want to go. . . . The act of worship itself requires individual effort and individual involvement."[5]

GETTING MORE FROM THE SERVICE

Here are some tips on getting more from a worship service, no matter what church you attend.

• Come to the service prepared. If you use the week before the service to live out Christian values, reflect on the Scriptures, and keep the Heavenly Father, His Son, Jesus Christ, and the Holy Spirit in your thoughts, you will welcome the time of corporate worship. You will have things to think about and your heart will be brimming with expressions of praise to God. But if you are up late on Saturday night and have not thought about God since last Sunday's encounter, there will be little fuel to light the fires of worship.

• Approach the elements of the service that relate to worship—the hymns, choir numbers, readings, and prayers—as a time to focus attention on God rather than on yourself. After all, worship means ascribing *His* worth. Make a conscious effort to express adoration, love, and praise to the Lord. If this is unfamiliar to you, you might center your thoughts on one attribute of God suggested by the service.

● Parents with small children are tempted to ship them off to nursery or children's church programs so the adults may give their undivided attention to the Lord. However, elementary-aged children can understand much of what is happening in the worship service, especially if their parents talk with them about the elements during the week.

● Use private devotional and family worship during the week to prepare yourself for Sunday. In the moments prior to the service, meditate on what you experienced in your own worship and recall questions you left unanswered. The worship service cannot be expected to tie everything neatly together, but in many cases it can bring you to the place where God can further meet with you.

● Present yourself to God in the spirit of Romans 12:1-2. As you worship God, allow Him to point out things in your life that may not please Him. "God is Spirit, and only by the power of His Spirit can people worship Him as He really is" (John 4:24). As you get in touch with God, let this spiritual communion take place.

A MATTER OF ATTITUDES

You could buy all the books on church renewal and the tape cassettes of sermons preached on worship and still find yourself apathetic in the next church service. To overcome apathy, you must work at it. Use the following items to help you focus your attention during worship.

I'm currently experiencing this need in my life:

_____

_____

I would like to express the following feelings to God:

_____

_____

I am especially open for God to teach me how to:

_____

_____

For the following person(s) _____,
I would like to intercede or request: _____

_____

_____

For the world in which I live I ask: _____

_____

_____

If you go to church expecting God to work in your life, He is more likely to meet you in worship, than if you attend without any expression of your concerns or worship goals.

LISTENING TO THE SERMON

Every pastor looks with chagrin on past sermons that really came off badly, and hopes there will be as few of them as possible. But it is not the occasional poor sermon that takes its toll on parishioners. It's the shallow offering from the pulpit every Sunday that tries the saints. When you've heard it all before and, perhaps, delivered it better yourself you silently ask, "Yeah, but what about_____?" or "That doesn't stand up to what the Bible says in _____."

In other churches, sermons may be over the heads of the congregants. In the late 1950s my wife and I attended the Moody Bible Institute in Chicago. We were both very young and had come from small country churches in Michigan. Our Sunday School teacher at Moody Church was exegeting the Book of Revelation. We didn't know what exegeting meant and we found it all but impossible to follow him. That didn't mean he was wrong to dig in as deeply as he did; we were just not on that level and needed a simpler class.

If you are not getting all you think you should from the sermons, try these simple tips. They should help you retain more and relate it better to your life.

Center on the preacher
What is the speaker's announced theme? _____

Does he seem to be talking about something different? If so, what? _____

What has he experienced that might have influenced his attitude toward that subject? _____

Flow of logic or outline.

_____

_____

What does he want me to do as a result of the sermon? _____

Look for spiritual content
What Scriptures are involved? _____

What do they teach? _____

What other Scriptures are applicable? _____

_____

_____

How does all this relate to me?
What lessons can I draw? _____

How does this satisfy the goals I set before the service?

_____

What action can I take as a result of this service and the sermon? _____

I still have the following questions about the material in the sermon or the scriptural content: _____

_____

You may not be able to complete the questions during the sermon itself, nor may you have an entry for every item; but the discipline of examining what you are hearing will help you see that the sermon is more than an entertaining experience. It's an opportunity which many people miss, to get closer to God, not only while the pastor is speaking, but in the days to come.

AFTER THE SERMON ENDS

As James advises us in his epistle (James 2:14-26), what we receive by faith needs to be translated into our actions. A bad attitude toward the church is generally the result of continually taking in what the church has to offer and never translating it into a changed lifestyle. The sermon isn't over until it makes a change in your life, or encourages you that you are doing what is right.

GUIDELINES FOR FURTHER STUDY

Sincerity in worship. Merely going through the forms of worship can never be a satisfying experience. You only fool yourself if you think you can fake a meaningful relationship to God. Sincerity is critical to fulfillment.

The situation got so bad in Israel, just before the Babylonian captivity, that the Lord said, "I hate your religious festivals; I cannot stand them! When you bring Me burnt offerings, and grain offerings, I will not accept them; I will not accept the animals you have fattened to bring Me as offerings. Stop your noisy songs; I do not want to listen to your harps. Instead, let justice flow like a stream, and righteousness like a river that never goes dry" (Amos 5:21-24).

Music. There is something about music that aids worship. You remember the words, often because of the melody, and you find yourself with this reverie for days to come. Often when other words fail to comfort you, the words of a song will. "Speak to one another with the words of psalms, hymns, and sacred songs; sing hymns and songs to the Lord with praise in your hearts" (Eph. 5:19).

Rest. It is possible that going to all this effort is going to take the fun out of worship. After all, the Lord rested on the Sabbath, when He saw that His work was done. For some, Sunday is a day to collapse—a time to think and do as little as possible. Others suggest that Sunday should be the day we offer our week to God.

Role of the pastor in worship. Various forms of worship treat the role of the pastor differently. In some churches, the priest guides the people to the throne of God, intercedes for them and offers prayers to God on their behalf. In other churches, each believer acts as his own priest, responsible for his own intercession and response.

But in every case, Jesus Christ is the High Priest who represents us before the Father. "We have a great High Priest who has gone into the very presence of God. Our High Priest is not one who cannot feel sympathy for our weaknesses. On the contrary, we have a High Priest who was tempted in every way that we are, but did not sin" (Heb. 4:14-15).

QUESTIONS TO ASK YOURSELF

1. Is the church important enough for me to keep working to make it a major force in my life?

2. What part do emotion and expression play in my worship of God?

3. How is a new attitude toward the worship service likely to affect my life during the week?

CHAPTER SIX
Understanding
Your Pastor

One survey of divorce among professionals lists clergy as
the third highest, only behind doctors and policemen.[1] Certainly the stress of the pastorate weighs heavily on those
who stand before us each Sunday. So much so that pastors
have earned a reputation for short tenures. Ministers themselves may be the most transient of all church members.
The Southern Baptists report that a tension situation or
crisis occurs every eighteen months of ministry and that
their pastors move on the average of every eighteen or
twenty months.[2] For some denominations the stays are
longer—pastors of the Christian and Missionary Alliance
have a tenure of three to five years. An average pastorate is
about three years.[3]

Few pastors reach the acclaim we tend to associate with
the vocation. Half of them spend their years of ministry in
churches with fewer than 300 people. In United Methodist
churches, two-thirds of the churches have fewer than 200
members.[4]

A minister takes a job with limited possibilities for ad-
vancement, as well as an unusual number of problems
associated with it. Also, there is a long line of people
waiting for his job, should he decide to leave. When an

independent church was recently looking for a pastor, its pulpit committee contacted Bible schools and theological seminaries for people who might be interested. They assembled 400 names.

Yet in spite of all this, most pastors feel a sense of accomplishment and usually remain in the ministry, even though they may change churches often. When I asked one pastor why he stayed in the ministry, he read 2 Corinthians 12:15 to me, " 'I will be glad to spend all I have, and myself as well, in order to help you.' It must be the pastor's heart."

When I was a full-time pastor in a rural church, I faced most of the problems and pressures faced by the average pastor. Later I worked as a magazine editor for a church fellowship and witnessed a steady stream of pastors flowing through the office to tell the director of the fellowship their problems and to share their joys. But it wasn't until I became a layman and watched pastor after pastor that I realized most of the problems we face in our churches stem from the lack of understanding between lay people and pastors. What follows is an attempt to open the door, if but a crack, and shed some light on the pastor's life.

LOW SELF-ESTEEM

Perhaps the greatest problem affecting the well-being of pastors today is a low self-image. While we may admire pastors for having it all together, they may actually be hurting inside and not know how to tell us about it. Louis McBurney, psychiatrist and director of Marble Retreat, a center where pastors, missionaries and other church professionals go to find new direction, commented on this in *Leadership*: "My experience has shown me that you can't really tell by a person's position, or by how he seems to be functioning, what he might be feeling on the inside. I've become closely acquainted with several very successful pastors who constantly struggle with a negative self-image. . . . While they've been successful on the outside, they never resolved the internal conflict of feeling that they have not done enough or done the right things. This is especially true of a vast number of pastors who lead small congregations."[5] Low self-esteem may be the number one problem that affects ministers.

Sometimes we push our pastors into roles that are not consistent with them as persons. To fill these roles, pastors may try to live the divinity of God and, in the process, deny their humanity. God is strong; the pastor should be strong. God sacrificed His interests for others; the pastor must subordinate his desires, even his family, for others. God was always in control; the pastor too, should lead the flock with wisdom, insight, and firmness. With this unrealistic emphasis on role fulfillment, the pastor is shattered when he can't meet his own standards. Then, if his parishioners don't share his enthusiasm or follow his advice, how can he have a good self-image?

LACK OF SECURITY

Former pastor James L. Johnson looks at a pastor's transitory occupation when he says, "A pastor has no contract, no assurance he will last a year in any given church. He is on trial from the time of his commissioning. Every Sunday morning and evening—and Wednesday night as well—he has critics in front of him. None of them mean to be that, although some are more articulate and vocal than others. But there is within the conscious territory of every preacher's mind the realization that if he doesn't 'cut it' to certain specifications, especially those of the opinion leaders, he is on precarious ground."[6]

The church I pastored in Indiana had the custom of voting on the pastor's contract every year. The pastor never knew, when September came, if he would be employed. Some normally minor or unusual incident could leave him without a job and a home, and with a tarnished reputation in the community.

DANGERS OF PUBLIC ACCLAIM

One hazard of the occupation lies in the distance between the levels to which the pastor is exalted on some occasions and debased on others. He has a certain image in the community which, if he is honest, flatters his ego. For example, soon after I had been called as pastor—before the ink was dry on the newspaper announcement—I got my first taste of what it meant to be treated with special respect. I was working with a group of teenage boys who were interested in what made cars run. I called a local garage and the owner said they had an engine we could have if we would just come with a truck and get it. When one of the boys and I entered the shop and asked for the engine, we were told by a crusty old mechanic in no uncertain terms where we could find the engine, and, furthermore, what we could do with it after we found it. As we huffed and puffed to load it into the back of the truck, I could hear the office manager explaining to the mechanic that I was the new pastor in town. Soon the mechanic was by my side, and in language as crisp as lettuce fresh picked from the garden, offering his help. I felt both insulted and flattered.

There are many examples of a pastor being singled out for honor. At civic functions everyone waits for him to lead in prayer. He counsels those who cannot work their way out of problems alone. He brings couples together in marriage and dedicates or baptizes their babies. When people who have not entered a church in years are about to die, they often call the pastor, almost as though his OK was necessary for God to continue with the proceedings. If he is not careful, he can become mighty impressed with himself.

But it is not far from the pedestal to the ground below, and there is always someone who would like to make himself look good at the pastor's expense. A longstanding friend of mine resigned his church of twenty years to go into evangelistic work in state fairs and other public ministries. The heat from his body had hardly dissipated from the pulpit when a church member from a congregation across town said, "Would you believe, I heard that he had an affair with someone in his church?" Even though such charges prove false, they can be debilitating to a pastor.

MARITAL PRESSURES

Unless the family living in the parsonage is exceptionally stable, it may find itself out in the street. Parishioners take a dim view of trouble in the minister's family. Yet the occupation itself invites trouble into the pastor's home.

There are times when pastors will flee to the church to avoid unhappiness at home. "I found the ministry a beautiful place to run away from marriage, because the demands were so enormous. Anytime my wife wanted more of me than I really wanted to give, I had to be at the church," said pastor Gary Demarest of the LaCanada Presbyterian Church in California. " 'Doing the will of God' is a beautiful hiding place. No wife can argue with that."[7] Though Jesus' words, "When persecuted in one city flee to another," are in the Bible, a pastor does an injustice when he applies them to avoiding tension in marriage by spending too much time at the church.

Congregants are often quick to criticize the pastor without realizing that the very gifts that make him a good pastor can cause him to fall. We want our pastors to be warm, compassionate, sensitive and caring people—all traits very appealing to women who are suffering from inattention, neglect, and even cruelty from their husbands.

No pastor in tune with God would claim his human frailty as an excuse for sin; but conflict at home and acceptance and praise from someone he is counseling can be an explosive mix. The sexual desires God gave him to make him happy and fulfilled in his own marriage can make him miserable when they entice him outside that bond.

Some parishioners are quick to say, "If he would take his

wife to the counseling sessions, that wouldn't happen."
True, but if he and his wife are feuding, how can they be
good counselors? And even if he can take proper steps to
avoid temptation, he may not always want to. Or he may
misjudge his own attitudes.

Some churches have a group of older women who counsel other women, leaving the pastor free for families and
men. But some churches have no older women who can do
an adequate job. Also, because they consider the pastor "the
professional," members may not want to talk to anyone élse
about their problems.

Pastors do not have to participate in sexual impropriety
to feel its effects. When former President Carter was interviewed in a precampaign article in *Playboy* magazine, he
uttered that now famous statement about lusting after
women in his heart. Presidents may get away with saying
that, but pastors—never. Most pastors feel they must set the
pace, be the model. Only a clear view of his humanity, a
sense of God's acceptance, and the support of his family,
friends, and congregation can keep things in perspective.

LIFE IN THE FISHBOWL

About this time you may be saying, "We all face insecurity,
temptation and, perhaps, low self-esteem. What makes the
pastor different from the rest of us?"

The difference could be that when we work through the
frustrations in our lives, it primarily concerns ourselves.
When the pastor faces the same things, it affects his entire
congregation.

"Perhaps more than any other profession, clergy families
live in veritable glass houses," says Charles Keysor, pastor
of Countryside Evangelical Covenant Church in Clearwater,
Florida. "Thus, what happens in pastors' families deeply
affects their total ministry." He feels that church people
look to a pastor's family for a model of what a Christian
family should be. Keysor says,

Our five children spent some of their most formative teen years in the big parsonage across from the church where I served as pastor for nearly a decade. After our children had grown, and we began to enjoy a frank, adult relationship with them, they sometimes revealed horror stories which had been mercifully veiled from us at the time. How schoolmates thought them freaks because their father was a pastor. How one crotchety old member of the church would constantly criticize them for not sitting perfectly still in church or for doing the kid-like things that normal children do.[8]

Many pastors have not allowed themselves or their children to seem to fail, fearing the reflection on their own image and the work of the church. However, such pastors sooner or later find that there is always someone in the congregation who will challenge their spirituality, no matter what they do.

PROBLEMS IN TIME MANAGEMENT

James L. Johnson points to one pastor, broken in health at thirty-eight, who said, "I never went to a ball game during my five years at the church. I love baseball, but somehow I felt that a day at the ballpark wouldn't go over with the church people. Still I needed a change of air. Every church picnic I attended led to some devotional from me and that continual public relations smile that is supposed to go with the office. I didn't mind that at all; I loved the people and those picnics. But I needed to go somewhere, kick off my shoes, and walk barefoot through the grass once in a while."[9]

The best advice I received in my first pastorate came from a farmer who was one of the church deacons. "Pastor," he counseled, "this job isn't nine to five. Buy your groceries during the day. Play with your children. Spend time with your wife. This isn't a factory job where you punch a clock." He knew that if I put in a full day, then went to the evening board meetings and special functions and cared for the counseling, I would soon burn out and be of little use to the church.

MONEY MANAGEMENT PROBLEMS

Most pastors I know are underpaid for the style of life they are expected to lead. We don't want to be ashamed of our ministers, so if they drive rusty cars, wear old or out-of-style clothes, or serve soup when they entertain us, we feel badly, if not a little guilty. We try to make up for it in other ways, but usually not in paying an adequate wage.

For example, churches expect their ministers to dress well. Many churches have what they call "the missionary barrel," a supply of clothing for those in need. The pastor's wife is usually told she has first choice. Any pastor can tell you that this is very debilitating. Knowing his family is wearing the cast-offs from the deacon's family damages the pastor's image of himself and his ability to provide. It doesn't help to know that the clothes are almost new—that the former owner just put on too much weight to make good use of them.

Few church members have any idea how it feels to always have someone else pick up the check, always to be the recipient of the "love offering". Many underpaid pastors spend far too much time wondering what someone is going to give them and how they are going to express their appreciation.

A friend who works in a large debt-collection agency tells me that pastors are some of the worst credit risks his company has. "They rank one from the bottom," he says, "just above barbers." Their salaries are too low. The philosophy, "Lord, You keep him humble and we'll keep him poor," is not amusing to any pastor caught in that syndrome. If I had not felt a love for the people of the congregation and a commitment to doing what I felt God wanted, I would have looked for a better paying job. My wife recalls, "I remember how much I wanted a pair of high-heeled shoes, but there were always more necessary things to spend our money on." My most embarrassing moment was when a man in the congregation bought me a suit because he couldn't take looking at my old one. Many pastors, especially in smaller churches, face life on the handout.

THE ABUSE OF PASTORAL POWER

What happens when the pastor abuses his power? One layman said about his pastor, "To hear him talk, you'd think he is always right. Sometimes misinformed. Perhaps a little bullheaded. Maybe even stubborn, and perhaps a little stupid at times—but never wrong."

With such people, the pulpit can become a pad from which to launch deadly verbal missiles at congregants. Though every seminary student is warned that singling out individual members for criticism from the pulpit is a gross misuse of the pastoral office, it is tempting on occasion, especially if the offender has launched his own attack against the pastor during the week. Outside of making a scene in the church, the parishioner is helpless against such an attack.

A more subtle way for the pastor to get the last word is in his sermon illustrations. "In our congregation, we have a man who . . . ." "You wouldn't think Christians would be capable of this behavior, but . . . ." All these phrases and many more have been used to cast aspersions on members who have offended the pastor.

As chief administrator in most churches, the pastor has the power of making decisions which affect his congregation in general and individual members in particular. In one church the pastor was unhappy with some of the decisions that some members of the board were making. He simply selected his own nominating committee so he would have those who were favorable to the kind of people he wanted on the board. Rather than stir up trouble, long-time board members let him have his way.

In another case, the board felt it was important to oppose the pastor when he wanted to buy a school bus and initiate a bus ministry. He raised the money in the community for the project and bought it himself. Soon the board and the pastor conflicted over almost everything. Within a year the pastor resigned, as did several families of the church.

At the heart of the issue is the principle of biblical leadership. Although the pastor is in the position of authority, he is called on by the Scriptures to be a servant to his congregation. Jesus told His disciples,

> The kings of the pagans have power over their people, and the rulers are called "Friends of the People." But this is not the way it is with you; rather, the greatest one among you must be like the youngest, and the leader must be like the servant. Who is greater, the one who sits down to eat or the one who serves him? The one who sits down, of course. But I am among you as one who serves (Luke 22:25-30).

MOTIVATION AND MANIPULATION

Roy Price, senior pastor of First Alliance Church in Louisville, Kentucky comments on why many people don't trust their pastors and other church leaders:

> Many times it's simply because they have been burned. Dishonesty heads the list of culprits, covering a large list of things from withholding information to manipulative techniques. For example, one pastor claimed a vision from God to validate a fundraising idea. His laymen had difficulty refuting the plan. They didn't like the idea, but they submitted with a wait-and-see attitude—how could they fight against God? It didn't take long for them to realize they had been manipulated.[10]

The same is true when people who have been giving to a television evangelist read that their money has been spent on luxury homes and cars, rather than on the spread of the Gospel message. Very few pastors are in this league, but every breach of public trust, no matter how small, has the potential for someone to shout "hypocrisy". The English writer Geoffrey Chaucer, said, "If gold rusts, what will iron do?"

Pastors usually feel responsible for the saints and want to motivate them to do what is right; but overzealous motivation is manipulation—and no one wants to be manipulated.

What is so difficult for most laypeople is the conflict of emotions that comes with being victims of pastoral manipulation and yet feeling indebted to the pastor for the ministries he provides. A pastor touches us at the most intimate times of our lives—when our children are born, when we face serious problems and need counsel, when our loved ones die, and when we make important spiritual decisions. A strong attachment bonds us together. An erosion of trust is difficult to bear.

GETTING TO KNOW YOUR PASTOR

The first step to improving laity-pastor relationships is communication. And we can never get to know one another unless we talk in relaxed, nonthreatening situations.

Chances are the pastor will initiate the first such meeting. It's called the pastoral visit. Though the mention of it may strike terror into the heart of the person who does not see the pastor except in the pulpit, the pastoral call is an important opportunity for you to get to know him, as well as for him to get to know you.

It is necessary to dispense with the stereotype of what a pastor is supposed to be. Pastors are individuals who rise above the generalization of a generation ago and who want to know you as part of the flock committed to their care.

When the pastor visits in your home, turn off the television. Dividing your interest is not only rude; it also deprives you of getting to know someone who may be both interesting and beneficial to you. If he arrives at a time that is inconvenient for you, tell him so. He would rather come back later than to put you on the spot or rush through a conversation.

Protocol varies from community to community. I pastored in an urban setting where I was expected to make appointments before each visit. I also pastored in rural settings where that would be taken as an insult. You just dropped in, anytime. One pastor recommends that a letter be sent in advance of the visit and that the church secretary call to arrange a time. Because the purpose of his visit is to foster spiritual growth, his letter asks for the parishioner to be ready to recount a significant event that recently happened to him, how he dealt with it, and in what ways the experience has been important to him. This way, when the pastor comes the church member knows what is expected of him.[11]

Other pastors prefer the less structured approach. If your pastor tends to this, tell him about your hobbies or other interests. Do not be afraid to talk about problems you are facing, questions you have, and the things that bother you. He wants to be your spiritual counselor.

A pastor is not just someone to get on your side. Many years ago a pastor told me about receiving a phone call late one night from a quarreling couple. They insisted he come right over and counsel with them. He dressed and drove to their home, giving as much time as he dared for them to cool off. When the lights of his car crossed the lawn as he turned in the driveway, he saw clothing all over the yard. The husband then ran down the steps and gathered his clothes which his wife had unceremoniously thrown out there. For the next two hours—until daybreak—each partner tried to get the pastor's side in the argument.

Learn to listen to your pastor. He not only wants to serve

you—he also wants your friendship.

Some pastors feel calls in homes do not get them in touch with enough of their congregation. One such pastor, John Weeks of Trinity United Methodist Church in Plymouth, Indiana, offers a standing invitation for congregants to join him in a dutch treat dinner at a local restaurant. There's no agenda, but conversation usually focuses on matters of faith. At last report, four to twelve people were joining him and he was thinking of going to two nights a week.[12]

ENCOURAGING YOUR PASTOR

There are times to share your critical comments with the pastor—when they will help him do a better job. But there are also times to keep your comments to yourself—when you are merely venting your emotional spleen or voicing a matter of opinion or preference. One pastor says, "About a hundred compliments for every negative piece of criticism keeps me on an even keel." He tells of one member of his congregation who says to him after almost every morning service, "I really enjoyed your message, but . . . ." "I wish just once he would say, 'That's great!' "

Here's a checklist to measure your level of understanding of your pastor and participation in his ministry.

YES NO

____ ____ I do not betray what he tells me in confidence.

____ ____ I am open in my feelings toward him and encourage him to be open with me.

____ ____ I am supportive of his programs.

____ ____ I try to provide him with positive feedback to help him in his teaching and preaching.

____ ____ I pray for him at least three times a week.

____ ____ I do my part to see that he has an adequate salary.

____ ____ I take his advice seriously and often tell him how it worked out.

____ ____ I am careful not to harbor hurts. When he does something that offends me, I don't make an issue of it.

____ ____ I respect his privacy and try not to make a nuisance of myself.

____ ____ I follow his leadership because I feel he has my best interests and the work of God at heart.

____ ____ I try to look attentive during the services even though I may want to drift off.

____ ____ I am regular in my attendance at the services.

____ ____ I occasionally call my pastor or drop him a note of appreciation.

WHEN THE PASTOR RESIGNS

One of the most difficult times for a church comes when a pastor resigns. Those who like him and tried their best to encourage him in the ministry are usually among the deepest hurt. One such man said, "We have done everything for the pastor. How could he walk out on us like that?"

Pastors resign for many reasons, and not all of them are negative. Sometimes there is a call to a larger church. Pastors have left a church to enter social work or become missionaries or take positions at the denominational headquarters. One pastor who was changing churches simply said, "I only have two years of sermons in me. It's time to start again."

Many of these moves do not reflect on the congregation—they just seem to. Here are some tips on what to do when the pastor leaves:

● Avoid the temptation to feel hurt or personally offended. You want the option to change jobs at your discretion. Allow the pastor the same option.

● Realize that God is more interested in your church and your Christian growth than you are. No pastor is indispensable to the plan of God. The day I was moving my family into a parsonage was the day that President John F. Kennedy was shot and killed. When we arrived at the church one of the grandmotherly women said to me, "There is no one so important that we can't get along without him." This is true about a pastor.

● Carry your weight during the time the church is looking for a replacement. When lay people who are not used to administering the affairs of the church take over, things may not run as smoothly. They need your help and patience. You may be asked to pick up some of the tasks that the pastor carried. Be cooperative. Stretch yourself a little and attempt some things you have not done before.

● Avoid the temptation to leave the church between pastors. This is the time when people who have been contemplating a change decide to make it. If several do leave, it can be debilitating for the church.

● Resist vying for power with others in the church. This is a time for healing, not for fighting.

● Sever professional ties with the former pastor. This doesn't mean to break off friendship; but it does mean that you resist calling him back for weddings, funerals, and counseling. A new pastor never feels he is doing a good job as long as he is overshadowed by his predecessor.

● Every church has things that need to be changed. This is a good time to reassess job descriptions, methods of operation and the structure of the church. Changes should be made before the new pastor comes.

● Give some thought to ways you can personally encourage your new pastor, particularly in areas where you may have failed the former one. Do you need to change your attendance or involvement patterns? Do you need to break some former habits and cultivate some new, more desirable ones?

GUIDELINES FOR FURTHER STUDY

Honesty and encouragement. When God told Moses he could not enter the Promised Land, He said, "Strengthen the determination of your helper, Joshua son of Nun. He will lead Israel to occupy the land" (Deut. 1:38). A verse like this shows the importance of encouragement. The real test is to know when to apply criticism and praise so that a pastor may grow and not become discouraged. Most of us say far too little of either.

The duty of a pastor. In the Old Testament book of Malachi we find a clue to the role of the pastor and his primary responsibility to the church. The nation of Israel had been in their land about seventy-five years after spending more than sixty-five years in exile in Babylon. Apparently they had forgotten what they had experienced as exiles. The priests had become corrupt, were not taking the Lord's commandments seriously, and were defiling the Lord by offering sick, lame, and stolen animals as sacrifices. The people, in turn, were withholding their tithes from the Lord and were divorcing their Israeli wives for the women of the nations around them. Things had gotten bad in Israel. God looked back at earlier and better days.

"In those days," says the Lord, "they (the priests) did respect and fear Me. They taught what was right, not what was wrong. They lived in harmony with Me; they not only did what was right themselves, but they also helped many others to stop doing evil. It is the duty of priests to teach the true knowledge of God. People should go to them to learn My will, because they are the messengers of the Lord Almighty" (Mal. 2:5-7).

How do you help your pastor fulfill his obligation as stated in Malachi 2:7?

QUESTIONS TO ASK YOURSELF

1. Am I guilty of insensitivity to the task that my pastor has, or do I share in his struggles?

2. Do I put forth effort to build the kind of friendship with my pastor that will allow for mutual encouragement?

3. Is my pastor approachable or does he, by choice, limit his contact within the congregation? What is my alternative if he does not want contact with the congregation? In what

other ways can I still encourage him?

4. If every member of the church had the same quality of relationship with the pastor that I do, would my church be a better place?

CHAPTER SEVEN

Serving in a Place of Leadership

Perhaps more than any other organization, the church cultivates leadership talents. However, with the opportunity for involvement comes the risk of failure. For example, my church serves coffee to the adults at the beginning of the Sunday School hour. Preparing the coffee is not a glamorous task and certainly not a difficult one, but I could get paranoid over failing at that job. When my wife and I are responsible, I set two alarms so we will not miss getting to church on time. The night before, I am sure the car has gas and the Studebaker is ready as a back-up if the car doesn't start.

I ask myself, "What's the big deal if I don't make the coffee?" Then I think of times when I've had to teach a Sunday School class of adults when someone has failed to produce the coffee. I've listened to their jokes about hangings and hit men. No thanks, I do not want to fail in coffee-making.

Providing the coffee is, of course, participation on an entry level. The risks for leaders with responsibilities for training, counseling, or directing people are much greater. One man told me, "How we deal with unchurched people is more important than the care a doctor gives to a delicate operation. If a doctor fails, the person may die. If a Christian counselor or witness for Christ fails, the person may spend eternity in Hell."

Knowing you *might* fail should not be enough to keep you from a position of leadership. Without leaders the church can never accomplish its work; as one of its leaders, you can share in the times when the church is successful. There is a feeling of accomplishment for the Christian who plays a part in bringing a person to Christ, helping someone overcome a problem, or making life enjoyable for others. Even little things—like watching people enjoy their coffee—give a sense of satisfaction.

By definition, a leader is one who has an influence, a following; someone who plays a directing role. We most often think of a church board member or church officer, but there are many others in a church who qualify as leaders— Sunday School teachers, youth workers, ministers to the elderly, and anyone who reaches into the lives of others. Churches need such people to carry on their programs and accomplish their goals.

MORE LEADERS—MORE GROWTH

D.L. Moody is credited with saying, "It is better to train ten people to work than to do the work of ten people." Having many trained people in a church will expand its ministry. For example, some churches have Sunday School bus drivers whom they call bus pastors. It's their job not only to drive the buses but to call in homes along their routes to enlist more people. Many Sunday Schools have contests where teachers are encouraged to build their classes. One pastor was encouraging his church in a business meeting to add another full-time staff member. "Don't worry about how you are going to pay the salary," he said. "My experience is that he will generate enough new people whose giving will more than pay his wages."

Involving many people in leadership is a biblical concept.

The Book of Proverbs tells us, "Many advisers mean security" (11:14). They also provide new ideas. "A person's thoughts are like water in a deep well, but someone with insight can draw them out" (20:5).

A voice in decision-making also promotes cooperation. Even when a decision has gone against the member's idea, he will usually cooperate with the majority. But if he has had no part in decisions which affect him, he is less likely to be involved in carrying them out.

Having a lot of people in leadership, especially on boards and committees, has its negative aspects as well. Committees can become so cumbersome that a great deal of time is wasted in reaching minor decisions. Recently a church shifted the responsibility for determining who should receive missionary support from the missionary committee to the congregation itself. What took a short time for the committee to accomplish took a long time for the whole congregation. Finally, after much time and much discussion, the congregation sent the same committee back into session to gather more facts on which the congregation could make a decision. Although this is common when group size increases, most pastors favor having as many people involved as possible. "It keeps me from experiencing the heat of a bad decision," said one pastor.

WHAT MAKES A GOOD LEADER?

David Murdock, pastor of the First Baptist Church of Wheaton, Illinois, looks for four qualities when he selects leaders.
● The desire to serve. The Apostle Paul told Timothy, "If a man is eager to be a church leader, he desires an excellent work" (1 Tim. 3:1). It is not wrong to want to be a leader; in fact, it's good. No amount of cajoling and coaxing can turn a person who does not want to serve into someone who will do the job well. A coach at the 1984 Olympics said he watched for a certain look in the eyes of a potential gymnast. Technique could be taught, he explained, but nothing

could create the desire to excel.

● Position in the congregation. People follow leaders they respect. Those who have shown their abilities of leadership over the years are usually first to be chosen for more responsibility. Sometimes these people are called opinion leaders because they mold the opinions of others.

● Demonstration of gifts. Church records are replete with cases of willing people making bad decisions in jobs for which they were not suited. I know of one man who has rejected several requests to serve in positions of financial management such as treasurer, auditor, and budget coordinator. Although he is part owner of a small business, he doesn't know a debt from a debenture, and his wife cares for the finances. But the church still calls on him year after year, because they see him as a successful businessman. They can be thankful he refuses.

● Involvement in church. Most churches do not think that it is wise to thrust people into leadership until they have been in the church long enough to know other members. People with outgoing personalities can accomplish this in a relatively short time. Members who never get acquainted usually make poor decisions in church affairs.

● Leadership style. John R. Throop, who worked in developing lay leadership in Episcopal churches in the south and now serves as rector of the Episcopal Church of the Mediator in Chicago, points to three styles of leadership. He talks about proactive, reactive, and interactive leaders. The proactive leader works on an individual level, initiating, taking charge, and directing the work. The reactive leader waits until decisions have to be made and then seeks direction from his superiors. But the interactive leader gets everyone's opinion and approaches the task from a group perspective. "Studies show that the interactive style of leadership works best in a church."[1]

Others may look for peacemakers when they look for good leaders. Disruptive attitudes and abrasive personalities make it difficult to reach decisions in a group setting.

The strife generated by an abrasive person can cause people to drop off the board or committee rather than face situations of tension.

Two indispensable qualities for a church leader are faith and concern—firm faith in God and concern for other people. If you lack faith and concern, your decisions may tend to be selfish at the expense of being spiritual, and they may be made through human intellect at the sacrifice of being sensitive to the Spirit of God. Achieving the right balance is a difficult task.

How do you know if you are leadership material? This checklist may help you determine your ability to serve the church on a board or committee. Fill out the first column; then have another person who knows you well fill out the second-opinion column.

My Opinion			Second Opinion			
Yes	No	Unsure	Yes	No	Unsure	
___	___	___	___	___	___	1. Like E. F. Hutton, when I talk, people listen to what I have to say.
___	___	___	___	___	___	2. When I see a need, I try to get someone else to care for it, rather than do it myself.
___	___	___	___	___	___	3. I like to work with groups of people rather than by myself.
___	___	___	___	___	___	4. I like sharing the credit with others, for something in which I have had a major part.
___	___	___	___	___	___	5. The ideas of others stimulate my creativity and bring out the best in me.

— — —— — — —— 6. I like to set goals, make plans, and evaluate.

— — —— — — —— 7. I am a peacemaker, helping others to work out their differences.

— — —— — — —— 8. I consider myself a detail person.

— — —— — — —— 9. I am patient, do not feel distressed when things move slowly.

— — —— — — ——10. My personality is perceived by others as nonthreatening and nonabrasive.

Give yourself two points for each yes, making forty a perfect score. Count *no* as zero and *unsure* as one. If you scored more than thirty points and are not serving on a board or committee, you should be. If, on the other hand, you scored less than fifteen, you probably do not work well with people in groups and would not make an especially good committee person.

HOW LEADERS ARE CHOSEN

Once a person has demonstrated leadership ability or shown that he has such leanings, it is up to the church to recognize those traits. Depending on the type of church, the methods of selecting leaders will vary.

If you are in a church with a strong congregational government, you may be elected to a position of leadership. The most common form of election is through the business meeting which is preceded by the work of a nominating committee. Perhaps that is what took place in the early church. "The twelve Apostles called the whole group of believers together and said, 'It is not right for us to neglect the preaching of God's Word in order to handle finances. So

97

then, brothers, choose seven men among you who are known to be full of the Holy Spirit and wisdom, and we will put them in charge of this matter' " (Acts 6:2-3). The church reviewed what they knew about the men, and either by consensus or vote, chose their leaders.

In some churches, the elders appoint leaders rather than have the congregation elect them. In a few churches, the pastor does the selecting and, though he may have a board that acts in an advisory capacity to him, he is the sole authority.

The Bible tells us of two more ways leaders have been selected. Just prior to the coming of the Holy Spirit at Pentecost, a successor for Judas was chosen by casting lots. The men prayed, "Lord, You know the thoughts of everyone, so show us which of these two You have chosen to serve as an apostle in the place of Judas, who left to go to the place where he belongs" (Acts 1:24-25).

The other method of selecting leaders described in the Bible is by the direct call of God. Moses approached the burning bush and heard God call to him (Ex. 3). Samuel heard the Lord call him from his place before the altar (1 Sam. 3). And when the Israelites wanted a king, Samuel told Saul of God's call, when he said, "The Lord annoints you as ruler of His people Israel. You will rule His people and protect them from all their enemies. And this is the proof to you that the Lord has chosen you to be the ruler of His people . . . " (1 Sam. 10:1).

Many people are suspicious when someone claims the call of God; there have been so many abuses of it. The call of God to be a prophet was confirmed by whether or not the prophecies came to pass. I tend to take a wait-and-see attitude toward those who claim divine authority to leadership.

If you recognize leadership abilities in yourself, you owe it to the cause of Christ and to yourself to develop your gifts. But you may have to wait for others to see those abilities in you. If they never recognize them, it may be that you do not really have them and are fooling yourself. You would not be the first to claim leadership without the qualifications.

On the other hand, not being invited to assume leadership does not necessarily mean you are not leadership material. I remember one man who had proven himself as a leader with a large company. His church, well supplied with leadership people, was not making use of him and he moved his membership to a church where he could serve.

For many churches, talent and ability are not always the prime prerequisites for serving as a leader. Some place a high priority on loyalty to the church. "If we feel this is God's person for us, we will use that person in leadership," said one administrator. "We feel that loyalty is more important than skills and that God will make up for any deficiency."

SERVING ON THE BOARD

One visible place of leadership is on the church board. As a nonprofit organization, a church is required to have a board to direct it. Though structures vary according to denomination and theological interpretation, most boards give some members responsibility for the spiritual welfare of the church and others responsibility for its day-to-day operation. The pastor, as a member of the board, shares in these duties.

It is this very division of duties and authority that seems to generate the horror stories which come out of some board meetings. Usually the conflict is between the pastor and board, rather than between board members. "In checking with fifty pastors not long ago during a ministerial convention," says James L. Johnson, "I found that forty-eight of them had never discussed what church authority structure they were accepting with their call. In other words, the pastor needs to know where he stands in the decision-making process of his church."[2]

If you are going to be on a board, be sure you know what authority the pastor has and what the board has. You'll find that pastoral authority focuses in one of two areas:
• The pastor as sole authority. Some pastors, with or without board approval, feel they are responsible to God for their congregation and that the congregation should follow their leadership.

They are not without Scripture to back them. Hebrews 13:17 says, "Obey your leaders and follow their orders. They watch over your souls without resting, since they must give to God an account of their service." In 1 Peter 5:2, we read, "I appeal to you to be shepherds of the flock that God gave you and to take care of it willingly, as God wants you to, and not unwillingly." These Scriptures seem to indicate that the pastor is in charge. How could he be responsible to God if he did not have this authority?

Paul told the church in Corinth that he had "given an order to the churches of Galatia," indicating his authority and perhaps the authority of all pastors. A pastor who operates this way sees himself as the guide to his board, if not its chairman. While he values the board and seeks its wisdom and cooperation, his decisions carry heavy weight.
• The board as authority with the pastor as a member. In many congregational churches, the board feels that it is responsible for the church and that the pastor is a respected employee whose advice is taken seriously, but whose decision-making ends with selecting sermon material and giving advice in counseling. Boards which have seen pastors come and go with regularity tend more to this view of leadership.

Pastors who feel most comfortable with this role see themselves as servant-leaders. When the mother of James and John came to Jesus to ask for favored positions for her sons, He said to His disciples,

You know that the rulers of the heathen have power over them, and the leaders have complete authority.

However, this is not the way it shall be among you. If one of you wants to be great, he must be the servant of the rest; and if one of you wants to be first, he must be your slave—like the Son of Man, who did not come to be served, but to serve and to give his life to redeem many people (Matt. 20:25-28).

A few groups, such as the Plymouth Brethren, have done away with clergy altogether; elders share the pastoral function.

A church can function efficiently under strong pastoral leadership or strong lay leadership. But when the board and the pastor do not agree as to who is in charge, hard feelings and inefficiency result. Being a board member in such a church is difficult.

Before you agree to serve on a board, it is wise to reach an understanding of your role. Some churches have pastoral and board job descriptions which set guidelines.

In addition to hearing reports from committees and determining what action the church should take in various matters, the board has to deal with power cliques in its own structure. Our tendency is to simply label power struggles as wrong; however, they may only indicate that growth is taking place. People want to be part of a good thing. When individuals push their own viewpoints, they can stimulate the board to positive action, if those viewpoints are in the best interest of the church. However, when a person or group simply wants to satisfy their ego or react to hurt feelings, you as a board member need to use every ounce of the tact, patience, wisdom, and sensitivity God has given you.

Confronting dissident church members is one of the most difficult jobs of the board. Most churches offer counsel but avoid directly disciplining members. Some churches do discipline their members and still maintain harmony. In many cases, however, the member facing discipline drops out without much comment.

The worst scenario is excommunication, which can have implications of large proportions. We're beginning to see lawsuits involving what has been publicly said about members involved in church discipline. As more of these cases are settled in favor of the plaintiff, we can expect the number of suits to increase.

SERVING ON A COMMITTEE

If you are in a church for very long, you are likely to be asked to serve on a committee. Here are some tips toward being a good member:

● Understand your committee's task. Committees do everything from preparing meals to gathering facts to helping other committees make decisions. It has been said that a task well defined is half solved. Defining well your committee's work will help you fulfill your function.

● Understand the relationship of your committee to other committees and to the church board. This will keep you from duplicating efforts.

● Understand your role in relation to other committee members.

● Do a thorough job. Whether you are preparing for an event or contributing your technical knowledge, give it the time and effort it needs.

● Be creative. There is usually more than one way to do a job. As you draw on your ideas, you'll be surprised what can happen.

● Enjoy yourself. That's usually all the pay you get for serving on a committee, so let the fellowship and the satisfaction be the benefit.

Serving the church in a position of leadership is one more step in bringing excitement back into your church experience. Being part of the leadership process is being a vital part of the church. Rather than waiting to be enthusiastic about your church before you serve, try serving and see if excitement doesn't follow.

GUIDELINES FOR FURTHER STUDY

Respect due the Pastor. The Bible gives us two reasons why we are to respect our pastors. The first concerns the work they do. "We beg you, our brothers, to pay proper respect to those who work among you, who guide and instruct you in the Christian life. Treat them with the greatest respect and love because of the work they do. Be at peace among yourselves" (1 Thes. 5:12). The second is that pastors work harder for supportive congregations. "Obey your leaders and follow their orders. They watch over your souls without resting, since they must give to God an account of their service. If you obey them, they will do their work gladly; if not, they will do it with sadness, and that would be of no help to you" (Heb. 13:17).

The call of God to leadership. Someone has said that leaders are born, not made. But there is a sense in which leaders are called as well.

However, most people who serve in the church do not have dramatic callings. Some have risen to the position of leadership because circumstances prompted it—like the kings who ruled simply because their fathers had the job before them. Most leaders are in their positions because others recognized their abilities and elevated them.

Once I asked the chairman of a mission organization how I could prepare to become a missionary with his group. "Don't wait for a magic button to push," he said. "Get involved." You can do the same. As leadership opportunities naturally arise, take advantage of them.

Extending the circle of leadership. Often churches are accused of being run by a small group of people who do not want anyone else to take part. Although that may be the case here and there, most church leaders want very much to share the responsibility, but have a hard time finding people who will agree to serve. They often feel that most other members are apathetic and that if the work is to go on, it must do so as a result of their efforts. Some studies show that the evangelism program of the average church is conducted by about ten percent of the congregation, no matter what the size of the church. Most groups, whether secular or church, which are made up of volunteers seem to fit the same pattern—a few do the work and the majority reap the benefit of their efforts.

While church leaders are feeling underappreciated and overworked, potential leaders in the congregation don't volunteer because they are not sure they would be accepted. Pleas for help do little to alleviate the problem. You can break this cycle by volunteering.

QUESTIONS TO ASK YOURSELF

1. Do I have gifts that would make me a good leader?
2. Is my personality such that I would cause tension in a church where I would serve as a leader? If so, how can I serve as a good church member without leading?

CHAPTER EIGHT

Responding to Tension

Roy served as a deacon off and on in the same church for more years than most people had lived in his community. His church was a little more than 100 years old, and Roy was nearing seventy. Occasionally the church had faced conflict, but Roy always weathered it well—until his friends began to avoid him. People he had known for years became critical of him and some were openly hostile. "He seems to be going in one direction and we in another," said a church board member.

Roy tried to continue his work as deacon but soon found himself not inviting people to church. Then he stopped going himself. Within months he was taken to the hospital and never came home.

Some said cancer caused his death; but others, including his doctor, said the church conflict took away his will to survive.

Many Christians face the trauma of worshiping in a church torn by tension. Their stories may not be as dramatic as Roy's, but the experience alters their lives. Some move on. Others remain and take a less active role. Others stop going to church altogether.

I have been associated with thirteen different churches—

three as a young person, two as a student pastor, one as a full-time pastor, four as interim pastor, and three as an adult layman. Most of these churches have suffered major conflicts sometime in their history.

Churches in extreme tension lose much of their effectiveness. One layman told of how he found it difficult to bring new people when his church was in difficulty. "When I tried to share my faith, people would say, 'Your church is having trouble. We don't want to go there, at least not now. You get *your* house in order and then we can discuss mine.'"

Churches in tension lose valuable members. "In our church we experienced a lot of personal growth, but also much sadness and lack of trust," says a layman whose church lost many members. "Other churches gained a lot of beautiful talent from us."

Lay people seem most concerned about the hard feelings generated by what members say about each other. As a result, some tend to withdraw from active service in the church and relationships with other church members become guarded.

Though some members work hard to overcome tension, just as many others become bitter and resentful. While some lay people may be drawn closer to the Lord, others experience a strained relationship with Him and may begin to question their faith.

Some people vow never to participate in the administration of a church again.

After going through a church split, "There was no joy in continuing to work and worship with those who were responsible for destroying a satisfying church experience," says one lay person. "I've joined a large church where personal involvement can be minimal."

One board member who went through a church division said, "I withdrew from personal ministry for about a year. It caused me to question God and the seriousness of my church commitment. I lost sleep, suffered psychological turbulence, and felt life was hell."

Conflict breeds more conflict. Once a personal attack is launched against the pastor or another member, things get out of control. "The primary problem for me," said one pastor, "has been the effect of conflict on my children. Some members have said cruel things in bitterness. The attitudes my children have could remain with them to some degree for the rest of their lives."

It's not unusual for people caught in the middle of tension in the church to translate their feelings inward. Headaches, stomach trouble and other symptons can result from unhappiness at the church. Do you remember a time you were at a church business meeting and felt anxious about a decision about to be made? Just asking a question could cause your heart to beat faster and prompt your tongue to cower in the corner of your mouth.

However, not all tension in a church is necessarily negative or disruptive. There are some positive aspects of tension. Confrontation may bring light as well as heat. Issues may be better thought through, arguments more logical, when the dominant position is challenged. "Many advisors mean security" (Prov. 11:14). Group decisions have the benefit of shared responsibility. People usually support decisions they have a part in making.

Although we may not like to think of this as positive, when churches split, new churches are formed. As those churches grow, they reach new people with the Gospel.

All churches face tension. "A church deeply involved in evangelism will always have tension," said Mark Brandon, a pastor in Mansfield, Ohio. "But if we obey God and spread the Gospel, then He will care for us."

It's not the tension that divides us but the way we deal with it. "We want to avoid conflict because it is unpleasant," says Jack Strating, a Florida layman. "Churches need to create a climate of creative tension that operates in love." Jesus never said our agreement would show the world that we are genuine. He said that by our love all men would know that we are His followers (John 13:35).

Carefully channeled, tension can be a positive factor; left to run roughshod over congregational members, it can be devastating.

WHY DO WE ALLOW DESTRUCTIVE TENSION?

If conflict hurts so much, why do churches continue to dismiss pastors, alienate members, and form competing congregations—over issues no larger than a personality conflict or a minor policy decision?

One reason could be that the laity needs more from its pastors. Laypeople are better trained today than they were twenty years ago. Many have had formal Bible training, or at least have taken correspondence courses or evening classes in the Bible. Church boards may have members with academic degrees and titles more impressive than those held by the pastor—especially if the pastor is older. This may mean a congregation is more likely to be critical of a sermon and less likely to be submissive to pastoral directives than in the past.

The church is a volunteer agency. When a layperson contributes money, time, and energy, he feels he deserves a stake in decision-making. If he doesn't get it, he may demand it. Destructive tension occurs when members choose sides behind leaders who can't resolve their differences.

As long as the church board and congregation follow the pastor's leadership, the church usually runs smoothly; but there are always people who lose confidence in the pastor's decision-making ability. Perhaps they think he should retire or bring new blood into the decision-making process. Since they feel out of order challenging the pastor directly, they lobby behind his back and muster support for an offensive.

Increased mobility has something to do with churches splitting. People change jobs, interests, and marriage partners more often. They feel less loyal to institutions, including churches. If very little stigma is attached to changing churches, people can more easily afford the risks of tension.

A few years ago I conducted my own survey to discover what causes church tension. Most of the pastors who responded to the questionnaire said a single person is usually responsible for creating conflict. That person has recognizable traits—he is probably between forty and fifty-five years old, male, and has been involved in the church for many years. Chances are good that he's on the church board and has been known to have caused trouble before, in this or a previous church. Those who cause tension are often people of significant personal accomplishment who are respected for their leadership ability.

Once when I was speaking at a church, the pastor made sure I had lunch with a man who was causing him grief. This man was soon to take early retirement from a responsible job. He had been involved in the church for a number of years and was on the board. He fit the pattern to a tee.

As we talked, I discovered that he was as frustrated as the pastor. He worried about the orthodoxy of the church, its failure to grow, and its lack of evangelism. His concerns were not only justified but shared by the pastor. Why couldn't they get along?

When I suggested that he simply change churches, he informed me that he had grown up in the church and that it meant very much to him. He had seen his children grow up there; the church supported one of his sons who was on the mission field. "I can't just walk away," he said.

I followed up several months later. The man still attended but did little else. The pastor found no way to make him conform or get excited about the church.

Several years passed and I inquired again about the man. After his wife died, he and several other families had moved to another congregation.

ARE YOU A DISRUPTIVE PERSON?

If you fit the criteria, you might even be the kind of person who could give a church real trouble. Without being aware of it, you could be a source of irritation to others and unhappiness to yourself. See if you fit the pattern.

● Are you outspoken? Are you similar to the rest of your congregation in attitudes, interests, and opinions? Though motivated by concern, you could be exercising a great deal of power, if you are expressing the dissatisfaction of other people.

●Are you short-tempered with people in the church? "People with quick tempers cause a lot of quarreling and trouble" (Prov. 29:22).

● Do you feel you are losing control and that no one in the church listens to you anymore? This is a real danger sign; you might create an issue just to test your power.

● Do you have a problem with a specific person in the congregation? One who is not at peace with his fellow Christians has a hard time being at peace with God or with himself. Rather than admit this and deal with it creatively, some people seek to center attention on a cause in the church, in a desperate effort to transfer their frustrations.

● Do you recognize distinct cliques in your congregation? Whenever a pastor or lay person begins to refer to people in the congregation as "us and them," he is exhibiting the early stages of the church-split syndrome.

ISSUES WHICH SEPARATE US

Not all church troubles result from personality conflicts. Some tensions grow out of legitimate differences about important issues.

What issues are important enough to cause laymen to stand against the status quo and risk alienation? Most pastors and lay people agree that the only justifiable issue is doctrine.

Both sides believe that if the other side would view the Scripture correctly, the problem would vanish. But doctrine involves more than just reading the Scripture. Our background, education, lifestyle, and attitudes all influence how we define our doctrine.

When doctrine cannot be agreed upon some people say:
- "Our pastor is not preaching the historic doctrine of the church. We need a new pastor who will."
- "Our pastor is preaching his opinions. We are not being taught the Word of God."
- "If our pastor were more spiritual, he would come to the right conclusions. It must be that God is not speaking to him."

People often hang their frustrations and corporate failures on doctrinal pegs. Some who say, "We are not being fed," really mean, "We disagree with the pastor." True, there are cases where large groups in a church have deviated doctrinally. However, many innocent people have been labeled heretics when the real issue was their methods, not their doctrine.

Most lay people who strike out at a pastor do so because they think they are right. But they fail to consider the trauma involved in spearheading a change; nor do they see the effect this will have on the church's ministry.

Unfortunately, a pastor usually doesn't learn about a member's unhappiness until it is too late, and then he generally hears about it through the church grapevine. Although a grapevine is often accurate, it can be slow. Sometimes a pastor learns of the problem from older members of the church who themselves are opinion leaders. Seldom does he hear from the disgruntled person.

Many pastors wait to sort out the issue before they do anything about it. This may take weeks or even months. Most pastors I surveyed advised confronting the unhappy church member earlier—when they first heard there was a problem.

It might seem that a person seeking change fights a losing battle, but this is not so. Of the pastors I polled, two-thirds left a church because of trouble. After the dust settled, more often as not, the layperson wanting the pastor to leave was still there.

HOW TO DIFFUSE TENSION

Because tension is a fact of church life, we need to know how to manage it. Here are ten tips for turning tension into harmony.

● Do not indulge in feeling sorry for yourself. This can lead to pouting and complaining to other members. The Lord hates a person "who stirs up trouble among friends" (Prov. 6:19).

● Appeal to appropriate channels. Every church has some structured way to deal with a difference of opinion, even if the grievance is between you and the pastor. Usually the first appeal is the church board. Select a member you know and talk openly. One church board member told me that only those people who stand behind their concerns are taken seriously. "If a complaint comes in anonymously, we do not even consider it."

● Avoid intimidation. Books have been written on winning by intimidation, but the Bible is not one of them. Still, when reason is gone, it is common to shout, threaten, and even bribe. Always beware of a person so filled with anger that he launches a personal vendetta. His arguments are usually weak and not to be trusted.

● Listen to what others are saying. If you really listen, you may hear people expressing feelings of neglect, frustration, or fear which may be far removed from the issue. You may also hear some new facts which will cause you to rethink your position.

● Don't expect others to do what you tell them just because you say it. One layman who played a major part in removing a pastor from his church said, "The pastor told me he wanted to hear my side of the story. We met many times but he never really listened to me." What this man meant was that the pastor never did what the layman told him to do.

● Seek forgiveness when it is needed. The practice of forgiveness separates real Christianity from those who merely profess it. When you let yourself become belligerent, you close doors that might have been open to reconciliation. If you will think of what God has forgiven you, it won't be so hard to forgive others.

● Try to separate issues from personalities. Write down the issues and pray about them, asking God to open your heart and to help you seek the good of others. Imagine the results of any action you consider, and project it into the future of the church. Many lay people have found that when the shouting was over, what's left of the congregation "rattles around like a marble in a shoebox."

● Ask yourself if there are other solutions to the church problem. God seldom brings revival to churches where shouting matches prevail; but amazing things are accomplished when people weep together over the issues that separate them.

● Don't overestimate your antagonist. Many people under tension read false meaning into what others say. Get to know the people you oppose. Don't attribute opinions to them which they do not have. Above all, don't assume they are out to get you. They might want the best for the church just as much as you.

● Place a high priority on prayer. It is vital for the Christian in managing conflict. Pray for an understanding heart and an attitude of love toward the person you are at odds with; and commit yourself to God's will in advancing the cause of Christ.

WHEN SOMEONE ELSE IS OUT OF STEP

Sometimes you may need to admit that you have stirred the muddy waters of church tension. At other times, you may see trouble brewing that has nothing to do with you.

Once at a church dinner, a member of the board turned to me and said in hushed tones, "You don't know what problems our church is about to face." It didn't take him long to tell me what they were. Within a year the church had lost a

113

sizable portion of the membership.

I didn't want to get involved in what I knew was to be an upsetting chain of events. And yet, my turning away did no good either.

In his book, *Management: A Biblical Approach*, Myron Rush says there is a scriptural way to handle conflict.

First, make sure you are dealing with facts, not guesses or hearsay. "Never convict anyone on the testimony of one witness. There must be at least two, and three is even better" (Deut. 19:15, TLB). . . .

Second, always make the initial confrontation in private between you and the person involved. "Discuss the matter with him privately. Don't tell anyone else" (Prov. 25:9-10, TLB). . . .

Third, when you try to resolve the conflict privately, if the other person involved refuses to resolve the problem, take someone with you and try again. "But if he will not listen to you, take one or two others with you so that everything that is said may have the support of two or three witnesses" (Matt. 18:16, PH).

Fourth, if the person continues to resist resolving the conflict, you may need to dissolve the relationship. "Can two walk together, except they be agreed?" (Amos 3:3, KJV)[1]

If you have to dissolve a relationship, be very careful how you do this. Some churches have found themselves with messy court cases because they have made public statements about an offender. Be cautious, seeking the best for the offender as well as for the church.

Just helping a person realize how his attitudes are affecting the rest of the church may go a long way toward solving the problem. However, occasionally, a person becomes offended, takes a position against you, and sets out to get even.

Part of our problem lies in the kind of people we are. We

spend most of our time in a world of competition and power-brokering. On the job, we compete for position, prestige, and paycheck. Yet in the church we are expected to put all this aside for higher values.

In a world with few models for Christian living, it is not easy to live out the character of Christ. But we can learn to handle tension in a Christlike way.

GUIDELINES FOR FURTHER STUDY

Unity in the church. The Bible refers to the church as a body in which all the parts work harmoniously together. "There are many parts but one body . . . and so there is no division in the body, but all its different parts have the same concern for one another. If one part of the body suffers, all the other parts suffer with it; if one part is praised, all the other parts share its happiness" (1 Cor. 12:20, 25). Paul's words seem to echo Jesus' prayer in John 17 that God would grant a oneness to His disciples and those who would believe because of their preaching. What can you do to bring your church closer to Christ's desire for His body?
The role of the individual in corporate unity. Church unity needs maintenance. The Apostle Paul advised, "I urge you, then . . . live a life that measures up to the standard God set when He called you. Be always humble, gentle, and patient. Show your love by being tolerant with one another. Do your best to preserve the unity which the Spirit gives by means of the peace which binds you together" (Eph. 4:1-3).

Make a point to observe the little things you and others in the church do that disrupt the unity of the church. Just becoming sensitive to the issue can go a long way toward building a plan for protective church maintenance.
Diversity in unity. How important is it for everyone to think alike? "Live in harmony with one another; be sympathetic, love as brothers, be compassionate and humble. Do not repay evil with evil or insult with insult, but with blessing, because to this you were called so that you may

inherit a blessing" (1 Peter 3:8-9, NIV).

Do these verses allow for differences of opinions? One saintly woman said, "We can disagree if we don't get disagreeable." If you were called on to set down five guidelines for building a oneness of attitude and feeling, what would they be?

QUESTIONS TO ASK YOURSELF

1. When I come across some information detrimental to the church, can I keep it to myself?

2. Is incompatibility with the pastor or a small group within the church reason enough to separate myself from it? How much do we have to disagree before I do something about it? How should I proceed, so as not to violate the teachings of the Bible?

3. I want to see the cause of Christ progress, but sometimes my own personality stands in the way. What steps can I take to become the kind of Christian I should be?

4. What can I do to stimulate unity in the church?

5. If I see another church member disrupting the unity of the church, what should I do? Do I act and react in Christian love?

CHAPTER NINE

Deciding How Much to Give

Although the subject of money has long been the focus of church jokes and sermon illustrations, it has also been a source of discouragement for many church members. One pastor put it this way, "Where two or three are gathered in the Lord's name, we'll take an offering."

"I used to support my church," said one man, "until they got to the place where all they did was ask for money." But it is not in the asking that tension arises. Church people know that money is important to the work of the ministry.

In the broad scope of charitable giving in 1982, the last year for which statistics are available, Americans contributed $60.4 billion to charitable causes. Individuals gave $48.7 billion; bequests accounted for $5.5 billion; foundations, $3.2 billion, and corporations, $3.1 billion. By far most of the money, $28.1 billion, went to religious causes. The next closest competitor was education at $8.6 billion.[1]

An earlier study revealed that individuals provide 83.7 percent of the money needed to run nonprofit organizations.[2] Such generosity is usually satisfying. The frustration in giving comes when the contributor does not feel his money is being well used. "Whether or not the donor trusts the credibility of an organization will have an increasingly important effect on whether the organization will continue to operate in the days ahead," says World Vision's Christian Leadership Letter. "Well publicized charity scandals in the past few years have brought about big changes in the attitudes of donors. They are asking more questions about where they are putting their money, as part of our consumer age."[3]

When there is disharmony in the church, giving decreases. If a church contributes money to a cause with which part of the congregation is not in harmony, offerings go down. If decisions are made to build when members think expansion is unnecessary, or if offerings are paying for the salary of a pastor out of favor with the congregation, it is not uncommon to see offerings withheld. This is one of the few ways an individual parishioner can register his opinion.

One major contributor used his offerings in a small church to manipulate the pastor. "I will stop giving and when others from the church come to ask me why, I'll tell them how I feel." Though few people would use their offerings that way, every pastor of a small church is conscious of the feelings of his top donors. It is not uncommon for a pastor to feel a tension between preaching what is right and hesitating to offend donors. Some pastors have gone to great lengths to keep out of church finances, denying themselves any access to the giving records rather than face the temptation to compromise.

WHY PEOPLE GIVE

If giving is a source of frustration for many church members, why do they give at all? Here are some suggestions:
● Guilt and gratitude. Psychological attitudes strongly influence our giving. When we say, "The Lord has done so much for us that we are compelled to give all we have," or "When we think of how good we have it and how much others suffer, we must sacrifice for them," we may be

yielding to the guilt/gratitude type of giving. Though compassion and thanksgiving should be the marks of a Christians, by themselves they can lead to shallow giving patterns. When the guilt is assuaged, or when we have given enough to express our appreciation, we can quit with a clear conscience.

When the local community club conducts a peanut day or sells lifesavers at a traffic intersection, I put my token contribution in the can, and place the premium on the dash of the car so I will not be asked to give again at the next traffic light. Many people treat church giving the same way—not giving till it hurts, but giving till it feels better!

• Token giving. In a church I once attended, a man approached the treasurer the Sunday after Christmas and asked for a tax receipt for his giving for the year.

"Have you used the giving envelopes?" the treasurer asked.

"No," the member replied.

"Have you paid by check?"

"No, but every Sunday that my wife and I are in the service we both give a dollar, and we've never missed a Sunday." The treasurer assured the man, who was employed full-time in a responsible job, that the church would be glad to verify his contribution for a dollar a week.

• Crisis giving. Unfortunately, much giving today, both to the church and other Christian organizations is done at times of crisis. Ongoing support for day-to-day operations is often more difficult to obtain.

The director of one Christian organization mailed a letter to his donors telling about the wonderful way in which God was blessing the ministry and reminding them that general expenses still needed to be cared for in coming months. "We failed to take in enough to pay for the mailing," he said, "so the next month I had to use a heart-rending story—one which was true. We were in debt again and without their help we might not be able to carry on. The response was much better."

It's not wrong to rally around a need; but if all our giving has to be wrenched from us by the wan child story, the foreclosure on the church, or the medical expenses for which the pastor had no insurance, we are giving for the wrong reasons.

● Giving more to get more. Many television evangelists and some pastors have given the impression that God keeps a strict balance sheet for us. For every $10 we give, He returns $100 to us. Give $100 and get back $1,000 and so on.

We can reduce God to a financial consultant whose prime goal is our wealth. We have enough problems with materialism in the church without the TV evangelists who say, "If you need a new recreational vehicle, God will get it for you. But be sure to tell Him what color you want."

God does not always bless our giving in monetary ways. In Romania, those who support the church the most often lose their jobs or are denied advancements.

● Tithing. The practice of giving 10 percent of take-home pay has long been the goal for giving. Theoretically, this works out so that ten members support a missionary, ten more support a staff member, while others care for the upkeep of the church and its programs. If all members would tithe, the financial worries of most churches would be over.

In Malachi 3:8-10, we read God's words to Israel:

"I ask you, is it right for a person to cheat God? Of course not, yet you are cheating Me. 'How?' you ask. In the matter of tithes and offerings. A curse is on all of you because the whole nation is cheating Me. Bring the full amount of your tithes to the temple, so that there will be plenty of food there."

The principles in these verses are also found in Numbers 18:12. The religious economy of the Old Testament was built on the tithe. Offerings for special occasions were in addition to that.

Deciding How Much to Give

Where the tithe began is unclear, but it existed long before the temple was built. In non-Christian nations, like Babylon, Persia, Egypt, and China, people were required at times to tithe both to rulers and as part of their religious duty. Abraham acknowledged the tithe when he met Melchizedek (Gen. 14:17-20). But the tithe was not only money. Much of the tithe was in grain and livestock, and in Deuteronomy 14:22-23, the giver ate part of the tithe with the Levites.

Later in the Old Testament, the laws concerning the tithe became more complex as tithing supported the priests and those in need, as well as paying for the upkeep of the places of worship. But the reason for the tithe was far beyond having resources to pay the bills. "Do this so that you may learn to have reverence for the Lord your God always" (Deut. 14:23).

The practice continued into the New Testament. In Luke 18:12, we read of the Pharisee who tithed; and in Matthew 17:26, that Jesus sent His disciples fishing to retrieve a coin from a fish's mouth to pay the temple tax.

There are those who say that the principle of tithing extends to the church today. Those who say it doesn't claim we live by the law of liberty; they do not believe there is sufficient evidence that the early church member paid the tithe to the local church as he had previously paid it to the temple.

On the other hand, the Apostle Paul wrote, "Every Sunday each of you must put aside some money, in proportion to what he has earned, and save it up, so that there will be no need to collect money when I come" (1 Cor. 16:2). He also talked about being a cheerful giver (2 Cor. 9:7).

Some who acknowledge the difference between Old and New Testament thinking feel we should be giving more than the tithe, because we have a more full revelation and understanding than those who were under the Law. "If they gave 10 percent," said one pastor, "we should be giving at least 20 percent."

As if there were not enough confusion, some church members attempt to solve the tithing question by committing themselves to the tithe and invoking a Faith Promise principle for anything above that. "If God blesses me beyond my ability to give 10 percent, I'll commit an amount or percentage to a specific project or individual."

Old Testament believers gave because it was the Law. New Testament Christians should give out of loyalty to God, because of our concern about those in spiritual and physical need, and because we are grateful for the salvation God has brought to us through Christ.

SOME PEOPLE SEEM TO HAVE MORE TO GIVE

Though we often talk about all the things we could do if we had lots of money to give to the Lord's work, few of us will ever have that kind of money, and fewer still would do what we talk about.

Having money is not evil, being poor is not spiritual. Many wealthy men in the Bible—like Abraham, Job, and Solomon—were singled out for their faith and devotion to God. Of King Uzziah it was said, "As long as he sought the Lord, God made him to prosper" (2 Chron. 26:5, KJV).

"The reason I don't have a lot of money," said one thoughtful pastor, "is that God knows He can't trust me with it." Many feel that God gives the ability for making money only to those whom He can trust. I don't think so. Generally, money making is a by-product of marketing one's labor and gaining on financial investment. Paul advised the church at Rome, "Work hard and do not be lazy" (Rom. 12:11). The virtuous woman of Proverbs 31 was characterized as one who kept herself busy by making wool and linen cloth. She bought land, and with the money she earned, she planted a vineyard. She was a hard worker, a strong and industrious woman.

This doesn't mean that people with low incomes are lazy.

Some of God's best workers have chosen to invest their hard work in areas which do not bring a high financial return. This does not mean that they can't be trusted with money but, rather, that their skills are not as financially marketable.

If you do not have a lot of money, it could be that you fall into one of the following categories:

• You have traded money for time. Many people view their occupations as a way to provide enough money to get along on, but not as a calling from God. If you are anxious to "punch out" at five o'clock and you spend a lot of job time thinking about what you will do on off hours, you could be nonoccupation oriented. It is not wrong to feel this way, but it usually does yield less money.

• You have a low pay/high service occupation. Those who serve other people, such as pastors, missionaries, social workers, and teachers are prime examples. Many Christians in service occupations may be able to give smaller amounts of money, but their human service is of high value.

• You are in a low-income or no-income situation. Because of lack of skills or ill health, you may be earning little. The newly divorced or widowed are often unprepared for the job market. The overqualified or underqualified, too young or too old, wrong color or wrong sex may at times find themselves without much income to share.

• You are in the normal low income/high expense years. There are times in life when giving 10 percent is about all you can do; however, if you are persistent in planning and in refusing to live beyond your means, better days should be ahead.

• You are a poor manager. Two-thirds of Jesus' parables mention money in some form. One of them concerns a servant who hid his coin in the ground and was criticized by his master for poor investment.

Richard Swanson, treasurer of the Conservative Baptist Foreign Mission Society and financial counselor to some of its missionaries, says that church members should set goals or priorities for the use of their financial resources.

—Since you are to seek first the kingdom of God, the tithe belongs to God first.
—Provide for the needs of your family.
—Care for your occupation. This may require investment in tools, training, or capital to make your business strong.
—Set aside savings equal to two to six months living expenses.
—If others are dependent on your income, purchase enough life insurance to pay at least five to seven times your yearly income.
—Own your home.
—Invest for special needs, additional charitable giving, and financial growth.

Obviously, this kind of planning does not bloom overnight into financial success. But it does indicate that Christians should think in terms of a strategy for money management. We need to be responsible in our giving, asking God for wise management of what we have.

DEVELOPING A GIVING PLAN

I believe that tithing was an Old Testament requirement and is a New Testament principle. Old Testament tithing represents a plan of proportional giving. Everything we have belongs to God; not a penny is rightfully ours. Let me illustrate with an exchange from a 1952 Jack Benny radio broadcast. Rochester told about receiving his pay from Jack: "Every payday Mr. Benny sits me down and explains how he has to make certain deductions out of my salary—so much for withholding, so much for unemployment insurance, and so much for social security. Then he further explains that what remains is known as take-home pay. He then points out that I'm living at his house. So he takes it."[4]

God provides for our well-being. We depend on Him, and

because our citizenship is in heaven rather than on earth; we live under His roof. What we take from our wages for ourselves is a stipend to meet our needs. God expects us to be good stewards of what we spend and to invest the surplus money for His benefit. Even the proportional amount that we give to Him first is to be governed with care—invested rather than spent haphazardly.

How do you determine a giving plan that is honoring to God and reflective of the fact that all belongs to Him?

● Examine your Christian values and level of commitment. Frustration may result if your giving is inconsistent with your level of spiritual commitment. If you are active in church, growing as a Christian, and involved in outreach, you'll hardly be satisfied with a low level of giving. Conversely, if you are not involved in those areas, even a high level of giving will not bring satisfaction. Most people give according to their involvement. Perhaps the following chart will help you see the relationship for yourself. Circle the terms which best describe you.

Commitment Level

Level	Church Attendance	Relationship to God	Outreach
+2	very active	close communion	active sharing faith
+1	about two times each week	close fellowship	share occasionally
0	regular	barely comfortable	only through set programs
−1	spasmodically	held at distance	occasionally
−2	name only	name only	none

As your relationship with God and involvement in sharing your faith grow, so should your commitment to giving.

● Begin your giving by setting a proportion you feel you can afford. Start with 5 or 7 percent and plan to increase as God provides and as you get a handle on your finances. If you see that your debts are growing, seek competent financial advice. Richard Swanson says, "I've never counseled any church member who didn't have enough money to give systematically. But I've counseled many people who were poor managers."

The important thing is that you honor God with your giving. He knows your heart as well as your needs and ability. Be consistent with your giving. As God increases your income, increase your percentage of giving. Perhaps this chart will help you arrive at a current level of giving.

Current Income:		Percentage of Giving:	
Wages	$_____	Last year's total income	$_____
Benefits	$_____	Last year's total giving	$_____
Subtotal	$_____	Percentage given	_____%
Deductions	$_____	This year's anticipated income	$_____
Total	$_____	This year's anticipated giving	$_____
		Anticipated percentage	_____%
		Next year's anticipated income	$_____
		Next year's anticipated giving	$_____
		Anticipated percentage	_____%

MUST ALL GIVING BE TO THE LOCAL CHURCH?

Many people feel all their giving should be to or through the church of which they are members. They point to what Paul told the people of Corinth, "Every Sunday each of you must put aside some money, in proportion to what he has earned, and save it up, so that there will be no need to collect money when I come" (1 Cor. 16:2).

Others doubt that all giving should be through the local church. The church in Paul's time, they say, did not have parachurch ministries, missionaries, and causes outside the church as it has today. Most Christian organizations receive the majority of their income from individual contributions rather than from churches.

However, you do have a financial responsibility to your local church. As it ministers to you, you should be sharing in the cost of that ministry. Most churches carry a clause in the membership covenant in which the member agrees to support the church financially.

HOW TO GIVE

While contributions through the weekly offering is the normal way to give, it is not the only way. Increasingly, church members are supporting special projects in addition to their proportional giving. I am unhappy with the concept of a church asking parishioners to mortgage their homes or go further in debt for special offerings, especially during a building program. Sometimes the urgency of outreach or ministry prompts such action, and usually those who can least afford it are the prime participants.

Planned giving through wills, trusts, and gifts of property is coming more into its own, as people make their assets available to the Lord's work when they no longer need them. Many churches and most missionary organizations can help you plan this kind of giving; contrary to the thinking of many people, they seldom try to build the organizational coffers at your expense. However, if you prefer, you can ask your lawyer for help. It is good to have him involved at some point, anyway.

Not all giving is financial, of course. When you give

counsel or a meal, you share as well. When you help fix the roof of the church or some equipment, you also share, because you keep expenses down.

HOW TO JUDGE AN APPEAL FOR MONEY

Whether we like it or not, pleas for money are a fact of life. Churches need money to operate their programs, pay for buildings, and support ministries around the world. Most appeals are legitimate, but occasionally, you may receive an appeal lacking in integrity.

As Christians, we are responsible for the money we give. I don't think God is pleased when we give it to an unworthy cause. Though churches are usually quite careful about what they ask of their people, occasionally they may take on projects more to bolster the ego of the leaders than to extend the ministry. Some churches have entered into extensive building programs before they were filling their present buildings, because they wanted to compete with other churches and make a name for themselves.

Churches seldom set out to deceive people. Even so, you need to examine the appeals that come from the pulpit. Are they worthy of money above your tithe? Are they going to spread the Gospel and change lives?

If you believe the need is worthy, then examine your ability to give. It does little good to take money allocated for the general fund through your proportional giving and designate it for a special project. Robbing Peter to pay Paul only makes another appeal necessary to meet Peter's needs. I know of one family which has a separate checking account just for the purpose of meeting special appeals. They know needs will come up from time to time which will need a little extra and they want to be prepared to help.

Sometimes sacrifice is necessary to answer a specific need and take advantage of an opportunity that may never come again. When that is the case, don't hesitate. But learn to distinguish between a real need and a bogus one. When a church or organization is continually making impassioned pleas for money, something is wrong.

You probably are on mailing lists of religious and charitable organizations. They got your name and address when you contributed, asked for information, sent for a free gift, subscribed to a magazine, etc. Or your name may have been on a list they bought or traded. An army of list brokers and direct mail consultants tenderly massage those lists trying to encourage new donors to contribute to their causes.

Before you support a parachurch organization, you need to know it is worthy of your support. You can find some clues in their appeal letters. Charles Colson, founder of Prison Fellowship and former White House personality under President Nixon, finances much of his work by direct mail. He advises, "I wouldn't contribute to anybody who says, 'This morning I was praying and your name came to mind.' Nor would I contribute to anybody who says, 'Give to me and God will multiply your gift five times over.' "[5]

Also watch for phrases like, "Without you we can't possibly carry on." "Your money is used to help people such as _____." "Think of the satisfaction you'll receive." These are all phrases which allow the organizations to use the money any way they see fit. I trust the time is coming when prospective donors will demand honest, simple letters from such organizations.

Even more important than what they say is what they are. Just saying, "I'm asking you to help me feed 100 more children this week," doesn't mean the organization has the integrity to do it. If you have seen the ministry in progress, know its doctrinal position, know its leaders or missionaries, and find it has a good reputation among the Christian community, you can probably give in confidence.

GUIDELINES FOR FURTHER STUDY

Giving and the quality of life. Some people give little because they don't want to lower their own quality of life.

Where did they get the idea that more money improves the quality of life? The man with two watches is no better off than the man with one. The man with one watch knows what time it is, but the man with two is never quite sure.

Yet the world around us influences our style of living. The desire for the bigger car, the more elaborate home, the more impressive vacation leads to injudicious use of our money. If we are serious about giving, we may have to live more simply.

"If you love money you will never be satisfied; if you long to be rich, you will never get all you want. It is useless. The richer you are, the more mouths you have to feed. All you gain is the knowledge that you are rich. A working man may or may not have enough to eat, but at least he can get a good night's sleep. A rich man, however, has so much that he stays awake worrying" (Ecc. 5:10-12).

Someone has said, "It is not the high cost of living that keeps us from giving; it's the cost of high living."

"Keep your lives free from the love of money, and be satisfied with what you have" (Heb. 13:5).

A biblical plan for giving. Proverbs 20 offers advice that applies to our use of money.

1. Train adequately for your occupation. "If you know what you are talking about, you have something more valuable than gold or jewels" (v. 15).

2. Work hard. "If you spend your time sleeping, you will be poor. Keep busy and you will have plenty to eat" (v. 13).

3. Be ethical in how you get money. "The Lord hates people who use dishonest weights and measures" (vv. 10, 23).

4. Exercise care in how you get and invest your money. "The customer always complains that the price is too high, but then he goes off and brags about the bargain he got" (v. 14). "Anyone stupid enough to promise to be responsible for a stranger's debts ought to have his own property held

to guarantee payment" (v. 16).

5. Build a giving plan. "Get good advice and you will succeed; don't go charging into battle without a plan" (v. 18).

Accounting. On what do you base your income? How do you decide where to give your money? Do you give a percentage of your paycheck only, or should you include company benefits and interest on investments into the amount to be tithed? Are expenses of your Christian service part of your giving? Could you count your contribution to a Bible school student's tuition? Do you consider the portion of your taxes that go for social security as part of your giving? Set your own guidelines, keeping in mind that the purpose of giving is to honor God.

Most of us will never have great amounts to give. However, if we invest well, we can make significant financial contributions as we grow older.

But what about those who have made more than enough to get along?

Command those who are rich in the things of this life not to be proud, but to place their hope, not in such an uncertain thing as riches, but in God, who generously gives us everything for our enjoyment. Command them to do good, to be rich in good works, to be generous and ready to share with others. In this way they will store up for themselves a treasure which will be a solid foundation for the future (1 Tim. 6:17-19).

QUESTIONS TO ASK YOURSELF

1. Do I have a specific plan for giving to the church? Does it lead to the tithe or already contain it? Does it allow for giving after my death?

2. How much money do I need to build a reasonable quality of life and yet honor God with my giving? Can a simpler lifestyle help me reach these goals sooner?

3. Should my giving all be through the local church? Or am I free to give according to the urging of the Holy Spirit outside the church as well?

4. How will I find out about a parachurch organization that is new to me?

CHAPTER TEN

Building a Bible Study Plan

We have more access to the Bible than any other generation has had. We have more translations and more copies of those translations than at any time in history. In 1984 Thomas Nelson, the world's largest producer of Bibles, sold more than $35.6 million worth of Bibles. Add to that Zondervan's *New International Version,* Tyndale House's *The Living Bible,* the *Revised Standard Version, Good News for Modern Man,* the *Reader's Digest Bible,* the *New American Standard Bible,* and the *King James Version,* and you have a multimillion dollar industry in the United States alone.[1]

Newsweek magazine stated, "No other country is as obsessed with the Bible as the United States . . . The Bible is a book more revered than read . . . . The majority of Americans may believe the Bible is God's Word, but they are not eager to study it."[2]

A Gallup survey of 1,610 adults for the 700 Club showed that while 15 percent of the people said they read their Bible daily, 30 percent said they never read it. In an earlier poll 81 percent considered themselves Christians, but only 42 percent could name the four Gospels.[3] Between 1963 and 1982 the percentage of those who believe the Bible to be the infallible Word of God dropped from 65 to 37 percent.

Mitchell Maloney, Pentecostal pastor from Detroit, Michigan says, "It is shocking to discover the number of people who have been attending our local churches for many years and who still don't know why they believe what they believe."[4]

The Bible is the believer's lifeline. The serious Christian interprets life around him through the filter of the Scripture. The Psalmist said, "As I learn Your righteous judgments, I will praise You with a pure heart. . . . Your instructions give me pleasure; they are my advisers" (Ps. 119:7, 24).

As a person reads the Bible and learns to follow its teaching, his life becomes more moderate and actually happier. It is not that God saves him from trials; but that the Bible influences his outlook and even his temperament.

Let's look at an example of how this works. One day I was reading Matthew 5:44, "Love your enemies," when I realized I had a dislike for a man in my church. I tried to avoid him, hoping to be perceived as being too busy to engage him in meaningful conversation. I had been hurt by him and I didn't like him. As far as I knew, my dislike had not affected him, but it affected me. I nursed the grudge and bitter spirits which became a source of private turmoil, frustration, and physical upset. When I thought of Jesus' admonition, I concluded that my actions were wrong. Practically speaking, I was hurting myself by my actions, also I was not being the kind of person I was called to be.

"Whoever loves Me," said Jesus, "will obey My teaching" (John 14:23). When you neglect to read the Bible, your view of God can be distorted. It's so easy to develop misconceptions. Today's wars, crime, abuse and corruption could cause you to see God as uncaring and cold. The financial appeals of television evangelists could give a view of God with outstretched arms, in some cases more willing to take in the offering than to take in sinners. Some ministers portray a God willing to do anything to gain your favor.

When you read the Bible for yourself, you discover the multifaceted character of God. Like the psalmist, you can learn something new about God every morning.

That doesn't mean that sound Bible teaching is not important; but teaching from others without studying the Bible for yourself can be confusing. It's wise to follow in the steps of John Wesley who said, "My ground is the Bible. . . . I follow it in all things great and small." In one of his sermons he said, "I want to know one thing—the way to heaven; how to land safe on that happy shore. God Himself has condescended to teach the way; for this very end He came from heaven. He has written it down in a book. O give me that book! At any price, give me that book of God!"[5]

WHAT CAUSES THE LACK OF INTEREST IN THE BIBLE?

Dr. William Marty, associate professor of Bible and Theology at Moody Bible Institute in Chicago, has some answers to why people stop reading the Bible. "I don't think anyone stops deliberately," he says. "No sincere Christian says, 'I'm going to stop studying the Bible.' But here are some reasons I encounter again and again:

● "The demands of living crowd out one's commitment to Bible study. Gradually a person spends less and less time at it.

● "Many people, even Bible school graduates, have not learned adequate skills. If you don't have anyone to help you and you don't know how to get the information by yourself, you can get discouraged. The nature of education in the church, for the most part, tells a person what the Bible says. What it fails to do is help him study the Bible for himself.

● "Sin in a person's life will also keep him from Bible study. Some Christians don't want to be exposed to the light of God's Word because they don't want to deal with sin.

● "Some people feel burned out. They don't think they know it all; but, especially if they've had formal Bible training, they may feel overwhelmed with all the study they've had. So they spend less time in God's Word than they should because they equate Bible study with other types of study."[6]

Writing in the *Good News* magazine, David Thompson points out additional hindrances to Bible study. "For some people the Bible barrier is a language barrier. They . . . find themselves drowning in a dialect far removed from their daily speech." He recommends a modern translation. "For others," he says, its "a reading barrier." For people who rarely read anything but a newspaper, the discipline of reading the Bible may come hard and continuing to read takes patience.

Thompson then points to what he calls a "substitute barrier." Some people "mistake reading devotional literature for the study of the Bible."[7]

John Oswalt, president of Asbury College in Wilmore, Kentucky, says a person must believe the Bible before it makes sense to him. "When a person has experienced the reality of God at work in his heart," he says, "it is less difficult to believe that the Bible is the Word of God."[8]

There is no greater encouragement to Bible reading than to find that its teachings are working in life situations.

ASSESSING YOUR PERSONAL BIBLE STUDY HABITS

If you have grown out of touch with your church, it could be that you first grew out of touch with your Bible. Here is a simple test to assess your Bible study habits.

Yes	No	In the last seven days exclusive of church or school:
___	___	I've read more than ten verses of the Bible
___	___	I've used at least one biblical principle in solving a problem
___	___	I've questioned a Bible passage and researched what it might mean (using such sources as a commentary, Bible dictionary, or concordance).

___ ___ I've quoted the Bible in conversation at least three times.

___ ___ I've been convicted about something in my life and looked to the Bible for help

___ ___ I've discussed a Bible passage with someone

___ ___ I've read at least a chapter of a book about the Bible or a related subject

___ ___ I've had personal devotions at least three times, during which I've read from the Bible

___ ___ I've kept to a specific Bible reading plan

___ ___ I feel guilty when I don't read the Bible

The old cliche says, "If a person's Bible is coming apart, he is well put together." If you checked yes only for the last statement, or perhaps not even that one, you could be coming apart spiritually. You quite likely are finding fault with the church and are experiencing a high level of dissatisfaction.

You are not expected to answer yes on all ten statements; six is average. Seven or more indicates that you realize the importance of the Bible in your life and rely on it for help in living the kind of life God desires you to live; but four or less could mean you are in trouble.

KEYS TO SUCCESSFUL BIBLE STUDY

If you are not making the Bible a part of your daily life, you might want to try regular study for one month and see what effect that has on the way you view the church, other Christians, and yourself.

If you have never read the Bible through in its entirety, consider doing so. When I decided to read the Bible all the way through from Genesis to Revelation, it seemed like such a large endeavor that I decided to keep track of how long it took. I'm a slow reader, but I never invested a better seventy-two hours spread over a period of several months.

When I read the Bible through, I saw the large picture of how God has worked with nations, how the coming of Christ is part of God's plan for our redemption, and how the various books of the Bible fit together. Martin Luther is credited with comparing effective Bible study to examining the shape of a tree. First you stand back far enough to look at the whole tree. You view the trunk and see how it supports the rest of the tree. Next you examine the limbs and notice how they draw substance from the trunk. Then you see the branches and the twigs. Finally, you turn the leaves over until you are familiar with their design.

Unfortunately, we often look only at the leaves. For example, you probably have heard Revelation 3:20 used as a salvation verse. "Behold I stand at the door and knock; if any man hear my voice, and open the door, I will come in to him, and will sup with him, and he with Me" (KJV).

However, when you read the verse in context, you see that it is not discussing individual salvation. Jesus is standing before an apostate church which has told itself that it has everything it needs. Jesus calls this backslidden church to come back to fellowship with Himself.

Reading the whole Bible through as you would read a novel draws the full picture so that you can see the verses in their context. You understand individual verses better and get a better grasp on what Scripture is saying.

DEVELOPING A BIBLE READING PLAN

Earlier in this chapter I mentioned Dr. William Marty. I asked him to recommend a Bible study plan. This is what he suggested:

● Set aside a regular time for study. Make an appointment with God and keep it.

● Write out a plan for six months and set measurable goals on how much material you plan to cover. Two chapters a day is good; but whatever you plan to accomplish, stick to it. If you get derailed one day, get back on track the next.

● Accumulate Bible study helps such as a concordance, Bible dictionary, Bible atlas, and a commentary. Have a Bible just for study so you can mark in it. Also use a notebook or diary to record your progress and applications.

Generally, study involves observation, interpretation, correlation, and application. (Correlation is cross-referencing with other passages of Scripture to check your interpretation. Use a good concordance and a good study Bible).

"Before you can apply any passage, you must discover the principle or eternal truth. For example, you can't directly apply Paul's teaching to Timothy in 1 Timothy 1:3-4: "I want you to stay in Ephesus, just as I urged you when I was on my way to Macedonia. Some people there are teaching false doctrines, and you must order them to stop. Tell them to give up those legends and those long lists of ancestors, which only produce arguments; they do not serve God's plan, which is known by faith." That's a specific command to Timothy. In order to make an application to yourself, you have to first determine the principle, which is this: involvement in trivial or irrelevant issues is detrimental to the spiritual life of the church. Once you know the principle, ask how you can apply it in life.

Marty spends half an hour to an hour each day in personal Bible study, aside from the time he spends preparing for classes. He feels he needs to be fresh and current if he is to keep his students excited about their Bible studies. "I will never say anything significant to my generation unless I have a message from God's Word."[9]

If you are just getting started in Bible study, you may want to plan for twenty minutes. Spend five minutes reading background information in a Bible dictionary. Use the next ten minutes to carefully read a chapter or two. Then in the last five minutes ask yourself these questions:

What did the passage say?

To whom was the passage written?
What did the passage mean to the original readers?
What principles can I draw for my life?

Finally, write down one thing you will try to do as a result of reading the passage. Be specific and be sure the action can be measured.

LOOKING FOR RESULTS FROM YOUR STUDY

Daily Bible study can't help but make changes in the way you live. Your Bible study should progressively become a source of strength to you. When you understand God and are confident of His care for you, you become less anxious.

A story is told of Eddie Rickenbacker's plane going down in 1942, leaving him and two of his crew afloat in a lifeboat on the open sea. They subsisted on raw fish and drifted through tropical sun and drenching rains. In the survival compartment on the raft was a New Testament. One of the sections they read was the passage from Matthew 6:25-31, which ends, "Your Father in heaven knows that you need all these things." They were rescued after twenty-four days, and Rickenbacker credited the group's survival to the strength they found in the Bible.[10]

As you continue your Bible study, you should also find answers to many of the questions that arise in daily living. When you need to know how to act in a certain situation, you can look to Jesus Christ as a role model. When a church business meeting is forthcoming, look to the Bible to see what God expects in corporate church behavior.

Though the Bible is not intended to tell you what to believe about every issue, it will build a strong foundation on which—with the guidance of the Holy Spirit—you can formulate beliefs consistent with the character of God. Issues like abortion, homosexuality, child and wife abuse, and nuclear war, have counterparts in the Scripture. When you see how the people of the Bible handled similar issues, you gain insight on what you should do. In some cases the teaching will be clear. At other times you will have to piece together information with which to solve your problem, realizing that other Christians may come to a different conclusion. But one thing is sure. You are closer to the solutions with the Bible than you would be without it.

When the editor of the *Pentecostal Minister*, a publication of the Church of God, interviewed three of their pastors to determine how to make Bible study a living experience, he found there was a significant correlation between Bible study and a successful church. "The fastest growing churches in America today are Bible-preaching, Bible-teaching, and Bible-believing churches," says David Bishop, pastor of a growing church in Yakima, Washington. "Emphasis on the teaching of the Word is not 'old hat'."

Mitchell Maloney, who pastors a church in Detroit, Michigan, attributes their growth to a consistent Bible study program. "The people's knowledge of the Word will carry them through life's roughest storms and will, at the same time, help them to lead others into the fold. As the Word grows in believers, the church will grow numerically."

In the same interview, Clyne Buxton, pastor of the Crichton Church in Mobile, Alabama and former editor of *Lighted Pathway*, agreed with his colleagues:

"A local church which develops a genuine love for Bible study will be a mature church. Bickering about petty things will diminish as the people give their attention to digging into the Word to discover what God says about living and working together. And as people live and work together in unity and love, they will attract other people, and the local church will experience growth. This is an absolute—the Bible tells us so!"[11]

GUIDELINES FOR FURTHER STUDY

Quality Bible study time. Worthy activities clamor for our attention. With family, work, church responsibilities, and personal interests, it might be easy to say, "I just don't have time to devote to Bible study, even though I feel it is important." We all think that the person who says, "You always have time to do what you want to do," just doesn't know our schedules.

But you can study the Bible more without setting aside extra time. Consider listening to tapes of sermons or Scripture readings while driving your car. You can memorize Bible verses while you have to wait for an appointment.

You could devote to Bible study some time now allocated for other activities. Exchange watching television for a correspondence course study. Rather than read a romance novel, read the Bible or a book about the Bible. Exchange half an hour of sleep for some devotional study. Commit yourself on a trial basis to more study of the Scripture; you may like it enough to make it permanent.

Most students of the Bible acknowledge that there are two kinds of study: factual and devotional. Formal study through educational classes or correspondence is one way to gain factual knowledge. So is Sunday School and many church services. Some pastors specialize in expounding the Bible well enough that their parishioners can get a basic Bible education from just listening to them Sunday after Sunday.

But devotional study is another matter. When you read the Bible and meditate on it to improve your personal relationship with God, the Bible becomes a living letter, rather than a textbook.

Application is critical to study. Wise King Solomon said, "The fear of the Lord is the beginning of knowledge, but fools despise wisdom and instruction" (Prov. 1:7, KJV). In the New Testament, James wrote, "What good is it for someone to say that he has faith if his actions do not prove it? (2:14). James gave an illustration which hits close to many churchgoers. Read James 2:14-18 and reflect on the times when your faith did not carry over into the right kind of action. What could you have done differently? How can you avoid making the same mistake in the future?

To engage in meaningful Bible study you need a plan. This checklist can get you off and running:

Regular time:_____

Regular place:_____

Bible study helps—(if you do not have them, try your church or community library):

_____Up-to-date translation of the Bible

_____Commentary

_____Bible dictionary

_____Bible atlas

_____Notebook to record your thoughts

Portion to be studied: _____

****

Day 1 Portion: _____

What the text says: _____
_____

What it meant to the original reader: _____
_____

Principles for me: _____
_____

Cross-references to other Scriptures: _____
_____

Action I intend to take: _____
_____

Each day, follow this guide as you write in your notebook. Review your notes as you go along and check your progress on what you intended to do as a result of the study. You won't have an action for each study, but you will have an application, most of the time.

QUESTIONS TO ASK YOURSELF

1. Without taking time away from family and friendship responsibilities, am I willing to discipline myself to schedule time for Bible study? Am I willing to say, "No Bible, no breakfast"?

143

2. In what ways will factual and devotional study make me a better church member? How will my study make me happier in the church?

3. If God wanted me to represent Him, would I know enough about Him from my reading of the Bible to do the job?

CHAPTER ELEVEN

Reaching Out to Church Visitors

Churches are doing everything to attract people—from advertising in newspapers to conducting neighborhood calling. But when they get visitors, they often find they cannot keep them coming. "We have about one new family in our services each week," says the pastor of a small Midwestern congregation, "but try as we will, we can't get them back for a second or third visit. What are we doing that's turning them off?" The answer could lie in the way they treat visitors—little things that set them apart, and make them *feel* unwelcome.

Dr. Russell Shive, director of the Conservative Baptist Association of America, put it this way, "Most churches claim to be friendly, but not many of them practice hospitality or express warmth to visitors. Time and time again visitors walk alone through the crowds in the vestibule and out to their cars without a greeting. People are lonely. They are looking for churches that will help them, that will befriend them, that will be sympathetic to their needs."[1]

Unfriendliness is conveyed in subtle ways. For example, a church I attended used to post a sign in winter months which said, "We will not announce from the pulpit when headlights are left on." It is bad enough if the headlight burner is a member of the church; but what if the person is a visitor?

Our lack of sensitivity is more evident to others than to ourselves. We often fill the back pews, causing visitors to be ushered to empty seats in front. Even if they are fortunate enough to be led to an inconspicuous row, they may need to climb over those who sit next to the aisle. How does one gracefully get past a seated person?

Once in the service, there is another hurdle—the visitor's registration ordeal. Usually visitors are asked to raise their hands or stand so the ushers can give them ribbons or tags to pin on or perhaps gifts as tokens of appreciation for their attendance. Even small churches where every member knows every other member by name and family history still make this observance part of the Sunday ritual. They may not understand how embarrassing it can be to a stranger.

"We no longer single out visitors in that way," says David Reimenschneider, pastor of the Bloomingdale, Illinois Alliance Church. "How can a visitor feel part of us when we ask him to stand and we all look at him? Our people say they feel awkward when they visit other churches, so those who visit us must feel the same way."

Although many visitors would like to avoid being singled out, others view it as a positive experience which makes contact easier for them. Here's what some churches are doing to recognize their visitors with as much grace as possible:

● The congregation is asked to stand while the visitor remains seated for a personal greeting.

● Members are asked to speak to those around them, requesting visitors' names and sharing something they may have in common.

● A roll card or form is inserted in the bulletin or placed in the pew rack. Visitors are requested to fill it out and place it in the offering plate. In some churches, the names are announced from the pulpit; in others, they are followed up during the week.

● A fellowship or registration book is passed from person to person within the pew. Each one signs it, enabling regulars to sort out visitors for a personal greeting and to link the faces they see each Sunday with the names on the page.

Though churches usually select a method they feel comfortable with, all methods are designed to accomplish the same goal—to identify those who are visiting that day. But merely identifying the visitor is no guarantee that he feels welcome or will come again. If members do not smile, speak warmly, and establish a contact that can be followed up later, the system fails and the visitor feels estranged.

Perhaps you have attended a church where no one spoke to you or shook your hand. Joan Martin and her husband experienced that cold feeling. After they moved to a new community, they visited several churches. Writing about their experiences in *Power for Living*, Joan said, "Often when a meeting was over we'd walk slowly out the door and to our car, but only one or two people would speak to us. On one such Sunday my husband looked at me sadly and said, 'It would have been nice if one of them had come over to chat. I miss the guys back home so much.' "[2]

Just saying "Hello, we're glad to have you with us," is a start, but it is not enough. Few things are more offensive than feeling someone has greeted you just to fulfill an obligation, without any genuine interest in you as a person.

Making visitors feel welcome is one thing you can do. And in the process, you may find your satisfaction level with the church improving dramatically. If you find that talking to strangers is awkward, and that you have trouble initiating a conversation, try a phrase such as, "I don't remember meeting you before. My name is _____." Usually a person will respond by giving you his name in return; if he doesn't, simply say, "You are . . . " and pause for him to fill in the blank.

We need more than a name if we are to remember the person. Faces remain, but names are easily lost, and most of us will avoid a person we should know, rather than be embarrassed by admitting our lack of memory.

If you can't remember names, you can remember something about the person, something to pick up on in the next conversation. Once names are exchanged, get to know more about the person by asking a question such as, "How long have you been coming to the church?" or "Can I help you locate a Sunday School class or answer questions about the church?" I like to say, "I am married, have three children and work for an advertising agency. Tell me about yourself." Avoid questions that are too personal—their age, income, or how they liked the sermon. The first conversation is not one in which to probe deeply or try to solve their spiritual problems. It is a time to lay a good groundwork for a meaningful relationship.

SENSITIVITY IN PROGRAM

Though personal conversation is a good way to make a visitor welcome, it is not the only way. If you are involved in planning the services, you must think about the visitor's feelings if you expect him to return. If you are on the platform or in the choir, look friendly even if your Sunday has begun badly. Have you ever watched people who sit on the platform waiting for their time to participate? How often have you seen bland, apathetic, scowling faces turned to expressions of joy and smiles when the participant leaves his seat to approach the pulpit? How easy it might be for those in the pews to conclude that we are actors more than joyful participants.

We've all seen pastors who were ill-mannered when they conversed with other platform guests during the service or stood closed-mouthed during the singing, failing to participate as they expected the parishioners to do. Once I observed a small group of lay people, most of them leaders in the congregation, gathered just outside the large glass doors leading to the sanctuary. The service was in progress as they talked with one another. I wondered why they were not more interested in the service itself, and in setting a good example for others. Undoubtedly, they had a good reason, for eventually they all returned to the service, but my impression remained: the service was not important to them.

The sermon itself is another opportunity to either make the visitor feel part of the church or estrange him. For people who are not accustomed to it, Christian terminology can cause them to feel uncomfortable. I'm not suggesting that we discontinue its use or remove theological terms from sermons, but simply that we refuse to assume that those who listen, especially those people new to us, know the terms and concepts so familiar to us.

Visitors may also feel unaccepted because of the language we use to refer to them. Do we talk about the *unsaved* and *those outside Christ,* which are exclusive terms? Or do we use inclusive terms such as *friends* and *neighbors?* Do we refer to our community as *our mission field?* If we do, we may be on the brink of we/they thinking which will filter through to visitors.

We must not assume that everyone in attendance has the same background. In one church I visited, the congregation was invited to a potluck supper. "Anyone wishing to come," said the pastor, "should let Mrs. Paternouski know." From the back of the sanctuary a woman—evidently Mrs. Paternouski—popped up and down so quickly she must have been on fast forward. The pastor smiled and continued. Unless we are going to rely on parishioners to seek out new people to give them personal invitations, we would do better with a registration table where Mrs. Paternouski could take the information. Many churches are moving in this direction.

There is much a church can do to help visitors feel welcome. If you are in a position of leadership, you just may be the person to make it happen. Here are some ways churches attract people and keep them coming. Check the ones you might urge your church to consider.

● Advertising. In your newspaper and yellow pages ads, place easy-to-follow directions to the church, instructions for parking, times of the services, and anything unusual about the church that the visitor would want to know.

● Signs. Information signs at the entrance to the church, directional signs throughout the building, and clear markings on restrooms, nursery, and Sunday School classes are a must. Parking areas should be well-lighted.

● Greeters. Someone especially alert for visitors should be positioned at the entrance to the sanctuary. It's important to tell visitors where to sit, what programs are available for the children, where to meet children after church, and any customs of the worship service which they may find unusual. If possible, the greeter should escort the visitor to a pew and introduce him to a member already sitting there.

● Follow-up. Most churches have registration cards or guest books and some churches have a place and time between services for visitors to meet the pastor. In the New York Avenue Presbyterian Church in Washington, D.C., visitors are invited to gather at the close of the service for a tour of the unusual stained-glass windows and a brief history of the church. More common are follow-up letters, a phone call from the pastor, or a personal visit.

If your church puts visitors' names on a general mailing list, be sure they do not automatically receive contribution requests. This can be offensive and give a false impression of why you are interested in them.

● Literature. A professionally done church brochure will be helpful to visitors. It should include a description of the church program, times of regularly scheduled events, and people to contact. Visitors like to see photographs of the pastor and other staff members. Listing the church's denominational affiliation is a must, and a brief doctrinal statement is also wise. You may also want to include some historical background and your program philosophy. Most church brochures are not lengthy. Visitors want basic information, not a book.

EXHIBITING CHRISTIAN CONDUCT

While sensitivity to newcomers will go a long way toward making our churches friendly, it needs to be accompanied by conduct in keeping with the friendliness we espouse. As Christians we need to create an atmosphere which says, "We like you and we like one another." Visitors watch as we greet each other. They overhear what we might consider private conversations and they observe the little things. Even how we drive in the parking lot is a testimony to what we are as Christians. I remember one church where the determination for quick departures would have caused Jehu to applaud and made Mario Andretti jealous.

As followers of Jesus Christ, we are told to prefer others to ourselves. Letting others into the auditorium before we rush in and handing an open hymnal to a latecomer are simple courtesies.

Ultimately, its members are the primary reason a church will attract new people. Genuineness, warmth, and willingness to take the emotional risk of initiating a welcome conversation will most likely make the difference between visitors coming a second time or staying away.

Here is a simple checklist to test how welcome you make people feel.

YES NO

____ ____ When I arrive early at the church service, I look for a place to sit where people will not have to climb over me.

____ ____ I watch for new people and make a conscious effort to introduce myself to them.

____ ____ I try not to stare at latecomers, especially visitors.

____ ____ I watch for opportunities to share my hymnbook or to help latecomers locate the pages of the hymn being sung.

____ ____ I watch for people who need help in locating classrooms, visitor desks, children's classes, etc.

____ ____ I always park in outlying spots, leaving preferred locations for visitors, handicapped, and latecomers.

—— —— When new people are introduced, I try to memorize their names so I can talk to them after the service.

—— —— I am conscious that I smile rather than be perceived by visitors as being unfriendly.

—— —— I try to sit in a different location each week so that I can get to know someone new, or renew an old acquaintance.

STRATEGY FOR FRIENDLINESS

Let's face it—many churches have become compounds where we carry on our own business, speak in terms best understood by ourselves and, in the process, discourage outsiders from becoming part of us.

But not all churches are willing to live with this. For example, the 1,900 member Old Cutler Presbyterian Church of Miami, Florida developed a program to foster friendliness and keep visitors coming. A few years ago, Dan Pinckney worked in the program. He said, "People fear a big church, because they can't seem to get to know other people."

In the Old Cutler approach, when a person enters the church he is met by two men and by a husband and wife team. The first pair greets him at the door to the church and the second at the door to the sanctuary. During the service, the congregation stands to greet each other and the visitors. A registration book is passed along the row so that regular members can see the names of any visitors and make a point of speaking to them.

"Various people take it on themselves to meet new people each week," says Pinckney. "They just pick out someone they don't know and introduce themselves."

Pinckney suggested that visitors be invited to a series of dinners held after church. "Each week three or four families could hold a potluck dinner. A long-time member and a recent member might bring the food. Two visiting families could be matched to the hosting families."

Reaching Out to Church Visitors

Part of Pinckney's job was to call on first-time visitors in their homes, after they'd received welcome letters telling them about the church and expressing gratitude for their attendance. He would telephone to ask how they heard about the church and to see when he could visit. Of the fifteen to thirty people who visit the church on a given Sunday, ten to twenty will supply enough information on the visitor registration to send the follow-up letter. Two-thirds of those are actually visited; one-third refuse the visit because they are members of another church, or have some other reason. Of those who come for the first time, about half are actually followed up in their homes.

Many churches do not have a staff person who can care for follow-up, and the job falls to the congregation. Any program will fizzle unless someone takes it on as a call from the Lord and promotes and maintains its efforts.

But keeping a person coming requires more than a visit to his home. "When we were considering which church to attend, we went to Old Cutler," says Phillip Capen, now a member there. "Our oldest son was the first to experience the youth program. He was integrated into it in about two weeks and, of course, that kept our interest in the church. Just having moved from Michigan, we wanted a place where our kids felt welcome."

Because many parents are more concerned about their children than themselves, the church that concentrates exclusively on the adult population may do so at its own peril. Not only do youth and children's leaders have the opportunity to attract parents through their children, but other parents in the congregation can make visiting parents feel welcome and wanted by helping the children of the new families become acquainted.

If your church has a program to integrate new people, take advantage of it; it will not only make visitors feel welcome, but will give you more fulfillment in your church. If you do not have a program for making people feel welcome, perhaps you can be the one to get something going.

ADVICE TO VISITORS

When you are new in a church, you can speed up the integration process. Not only are you looking for certain things in a church; the church may be looking for certain things in you. Bill and his family were looking for a church in the suburb of a large city. "As soon as people in the church found that I had been active in my former church, acceptance was natural," he says. But Bill did more than wait for acceptance. He initiated conversations with people. After he was satisfied with the doctrinal position of the church, he and his family quickly applied for membership. He volunteered for jobs matched to his abilities and engaged in discussion on church matters. In short, he took the initiative. "If you prove yourself to be friendly, everyone will seem to be friendly. If you are not outgoing and friendly yourself, then others won't seem to be friendly, either," he says.

Newcomers may *feel* more estrangement than actually exists in a church and may be hesitant to attend functions of the church and Sunday School. When they don't attend, they cut off a vital means of becoming acquainted and finding acceptance. In smaller groups, such as Sunday School parties or clean-up days, the individual is more visible and will become acquainted with others more quickly. But the new person has to take the initiative.

GUIDELINES FOR FURTHER STUDY

Overcoming Apprehension. While friendliness has to be worked at, isolation happens naturally. An early church leader named Ananias was told to visit Saul, who had been imprisoning Christians. Though the Bible doesn't tell us, I imagine when the Lord ordered him to go to Saul, Ananias was apprehensive. He told the Lord what Saul had done to the church, as if he wanted to be sure that God really wanted him to go make the call. "The Lord said to him, 'Go because I have chosen him to serve Me' " (Acts 9:15).

Ananias could have felt reluctant to let Saul know about himself or the state of the church, for according to Saul's past behavior, the danger was very real. Although we probably will never feel the apprehensions of Ananias, we sometimes act as if we are not really sure we want new people to be part of our group. How great it is to conquer our fears and say with Ananias, "The Lord has sent me" (Acts 9:17). We may find that the Lord has sent the visitor to bless us as well.

Finding Social and Spiritual Acceptance. People who are easy to talk to receive our attention. Those most different from us are often left to fend for themselves. Economic status, social similarities, church background and age send signals to us that a conversation will either be comfortable or threatening. Unless we deliberately override them, these signals govern how friendly we will be.

This is unfortunate, because those most difficult for us to approach often make the best contributions to our lives. At a conference of Christian media personnel my wife and I attended, we found we were spending most of our time with people we already knew. A small group of editors we had not met stood apart from the group. Some of their hair and clothing styles were Punk—even bizarre—compared to the rest of the conferees. "We should sit with them at lunch and get to know them," my wife said. When the opportunity presented itself, we did and found the conversation friendly, enlightening, and fulfilling. We learned a lot about their life and ministry and gained some new friends. To our surprise, we found that they had been praying about younger people entering their community. "At first we rejected these kids who wore leather jackets embedded with studs," said one of the editors. "Then we remembered what life had been for us when we were that age, and we saw God move among us."

Several months later we met the same group at a printers' trade show in Chicago. I was happy to see them and we exchanged Christian greetings. As they walked about the displays, I could see other people avoiding them. By that time I knew what the others were missing.

In the church it's the kid without clean clothing or the fat or short or handicapped person who is left alone. Those we exclude because we find them unlike ourselves may suffer because of it, but we suffer too. Do yourself a favor and initiate a conversation. You'll be glad you did. If you're worried about what other people will think, consider carefully how much you should value the opinion of those nebulous "other people." You may surprise yourself with your answer.

QUESTIONS TO ASK YOURSELF

1. Do I really want more people to come to the church I attend? If so, why? To minister to them? So our church will grow? So I may grow by meeting them? To infuse new ideas into the church?

2. Am I willing to take the trouble to make others feel welcome? Is it worth the risk of their possible rejection of me?

3. How would I feel if I were in a church where no one other than the professional greeters talked to me?

4. What can I do to encourage friendliness in my church?

CHAPTER TWELVE

Knowing When to Change Churches

Each year people of all denominations change churches, and for many reasons: job transfer, moving to a new home, helping to start a new church in the area, being useful to a struggling congregation, retiring to a new part of the country, getting married or divorced, for the sake of their children, or because of dissatisfaction with the present church.

The Religious News Service reports that mainline Protestant denominations have lost millions of members since the mid-1960s. Although that trend seems to be reversing in the early 1980s, church growth still lags behind the natural population increase. Growth for theologically conservative churches seems to be slowing down as mainline churches begin to increase. Denominational reports for 1982 showed United Methodists, Lutheran Church (Missouri Synod), United Church of Christ, and Disciples of Christ all to be down. Catholics, Southern Baptists and Assemblies of God were growing.[1]

Though changing churches may look easy, the move is not all that pleasant. Even if necessitated by the purchase of a new home or a job transfer, it means leaving old friends and establishing new ones. "Will I like them? Will they like me? Will they do things differently?"

If the move is precipitated by unhappiness in the present church, it can be especially unsettling. Long-time friends may perceive your action as an insult to them. Some may wonder why you no longer like them or what they did to make you unhappy.

One pastor friend of mine found changing churches to be especially traumatic. He had been the chairman of his church board before being asked to be their pastor. Now, four years later, because of a dispute in the church, he was leaving. Where was he to go to church? He was not leaving the area, but was going into business for himself in the same town. Though he had been in that church for eighteen years, he could no longer attend there because of the threat he would pose to the incoming pastor. As he visited small churches in the area, their pastors also seemed threatened by his presence and his standing in the religious community. It seemed his only choices were denominations quite removed from his own or very large churches which were some distance. The change would not be easy.

We can understand this pastor's precarious position, for lay people face similar feelings. When Deborah Brunt was faced with the possibilities of a church change, she wrote in *Moody Monthly*, "Pastor Brown preached the truth. He believed the Bible, but he had chosen the shallow water for so long that those who stayed awake during his sermons could predict where he was going.

"Church attendance began to fall off, slowly at first, and then sharply. Gaps appeared in our ranks of teachers and leaders. Without warning, key members began to move their membership. . . . Nagging questions now surfaced. What's wrong with us?"[2]

APPROPRIATE REASONS FOR CHANGE

When circumstances such as job relocation or marriage necessitate a church change, everyone understands. The difficult change is when you continue to live in the same area but choose to attend a different church. Finding a new congregation with which to worship may give you a new start, but if you bring your old problems with you, the satisfaction will be only temporary. If you are convinced that the problem is not within yourself and if you have prayed about the matter and feel free to make the move, it may be a reasonable option.

Here are some times when changing churches may be in order:

● The church has changed doctrinal positions and is no longer true to the teachings of the Bible. Some churches that once were faithful to the Scriptures no longer hold to such doctrines as the virgin birth, inspiration of the Scriptures, or salvation by faith. The late Francis Schaeffer said, "If the battle for doctrinal purity is lost . . . it may be necessary for true Christians to leave the visible organization with which they have been associated. But note well: if we must leave our church, it should always be with tears— not with drums playing and flags flying. This is no place for naturally bombastic men to bombast."

One word of caution, however. Not everyone who shouts, "Heresy, Heresy," has a case. Some people have voiced their personal grievances in doctrinal terms. I've heard more people than I can count complain about their pastor with the phrase, "He doesn't preach the Word anymore."

● Tension in the church becomes so strong that the community outside is getting the idea that somehow being unsaved is closer to God than being a member of that particular church. Usually the problems that churches have can be solved if some way to develop understanding can be found. Most of the members of the church and the church staff have the same goals: reaching and helping people and exalting the Lord. If they can communicate their ideas to one another and pray together, very often they can resolve differences and get on toward their goals. You should try to foster understanding and work your differences out before you settle on changing churches. If you leave in defeat, you will always have a poor attitude toward that particular church. But if you can work out differences, relationships are cemented and positive attitudes result.

Not all tension can be handled through communication. President Kennedy was once asked in a press conference if he had made any progress in establishing a direct telephone line to the Kremlin. "We have communication with the Soviet Union," Kennedy replied. "I think that the problem is not communication. The problem is that there is a difference of viewpoint. We understand each other, but we differ."

The church has its times of differing as well. When you realize that you must hold your position, even though it is opposed by many others in the church, your presence may be divisive. You have four options: direct the church to your thinking, shift your opinions to agree with the rest of the congregation, take the loss of your way in stride as you agree to go along with the decision, or withdraw from the church.

You can't always be right and sometimes you are dead wrong. Often it doesn't make any difference. The object is not winning, but doing the Christlike thing by yielding your interests to the good of the group and the cause of Christ. When you see that you are creating tension, it is time to consider the alternatives; leaving is one of them.

I remember a neighborhood dog that loved to chase cars. I often wondered what he would do if he caught one. I've seen church members with as much determination as that dog to get their own way. And I've seen them hover over a nearly empty building with only a few followers, once they had "won." Not only did they hurt many others, but they too suffered in the chase. In many of these cases, it would have been better if they had sought out another church in which to worship, one where they were more appreciated.

● Your needs or those of your family have changed to the point that your present church can no longer meet them. Some church members and leaders criticize this thinking as selfish. They say, "You shouldn't ask what you can get from the church, but should ask what you can do for the church." That's true in many stages in our lives; but there are times when we are not serving the church enough to stay and the church is not serving us enough to keep us from leaving.

For example, the single person in a church of married people finds his social needs are not met, and no degree of good preaching can help. Since not all churches seek to provide something for everyone—and they shouldn't—it is not wrong for the single person to hunt for a church with that kind of ministry as long as it doesn't call for a compromise in doctrine or allegiance to God. And the same can be true for young marrieds, retired persons, and those just out of high school but not bound for college.

If you and the church can't get together, you may find another church more suited to you. It is not wrong to leave a church, but it is wrong to leave without first giving the church a chance to minister to you and also giving yourself an opportunity to think through the results of a possible move.

WHEN IT'S NOT TIME TO CHANGE CHURCHES

Far too many people change churches for the wrong reasons. When criticized, or excluded from some event or office, when asked to do too much or too little, when the preaching disagrees with them, when some other church hires a pastor whom they think they will like better, when they find a boyfriend or a girlfriend, when another church has better music, or a bigger building or a more active program.

● Don't change churches if it necessitates a doctrinal compromise. Sacrificing your convictions and beliefs to meet social needs or to find a place to serve is too great a price to pay.

Some people have said, "So what if the church is not teaching the Bible? The people are friendly and caring." Yet, in a large measure, doctrine determines our behavior. James makes the connection when he says, "Show me how anyone can have faith without actions. I will show you my faith by my actions" (James 2:18).

● Don't change churches just because your personality clashes with a church member or the pastor. In a Sunday School class I once taught, there were three men who seemed critical about what I was teaching. I struggled through the first two sessions and seriously considered whether I would ever teach that class again if I were asked—which I doubted. On the third Sunday of the quarter all three men, unsolicited and unknown to the others, remarked how much they liked the class. It's easy to perceive exclusion or conflict when none exists.

Sometimes the conflict *is* genuine. When this happens, look for ways to work out personality differences. Use conversational opportunities to gain understanding. You may find that you still don't like the people involved, but you will run into this in any church you attend. Part of being the universal family of God is that we are all in the growing process.

● Don't change churches when your personal life is at a low ebb or when you have a problem with sin. Though I have seen churches with high standards for themselves and for their parishioners, I have never seen a church that was opposed to helping a member who had a personal or spiritual problem.

You need the church when you face problems; that's part of the family concept of the church. If you change churches, be assured your problems will follow. A move may be a way to take your mind off your troubles for awhile, but they will soon make their presence known. Solve them in your present church where people know and accept you, rather than calling on strangers who will be less understanding and perhaps less forgiving.

162

HOW TO CHANGE CHURCHES

Leaving a church is not as simple as you might think, and few people seem to know how to make the change without engendering some ill feelings. If you find it necessary to make a change, here are six suggestions to make the transition go more smoothly.

● Do everything you can to maintain your personal integrity. It's tempting to want to prove a point or make a statement of what is wrong with the church before you leave, but to do so you may have to sacrifice your integrity. Ask yourself, "When I am gone, how do I want to be remembered?" For your good and the good of the church, it is important to maintain Christian character and show concern for the rest of the church.

● Fulfill the responsibilities to which you obligated yourself. Plan your leaving to coincide with times when you have few responsibilities, such as the end of the teaching year if you are a Sunday School teacher. Your students may not remember all you taught, but they will remember your attitude toward your responsibilties.

● Make the announcement to the pastor first, especially if the church is small and you know him well. A pastor often feels personally offended when people leave the congregation, even though the reason may not involve him. Be honest but not vindictive; and remember that as the person leaving you are in control—you are not there to argue, only to inform him.

You can get some help from John 16 in Jesus' words to His disciples in the Upper Room, before He was to leave them. Treat the announcement factually. Though His departure would be through death, Jesus refused to make an emotional announcement. He simply stated to those gathered, "In a little while you will not see Me anymore," yet He understood the implications, for He went on to say, "You will cry and weep, but the world will be glad; you will be sad, but your sadness will turn into gladness" (vv. 16, 20).

Though it might not be appropriate to use Jesus' words, you can simply say, "We have decided that it is time for us to make a change. We've appreciated your friendship and hope it will remain."

● Remember that though there is sadness now, it will pass. In the same passage Jesus told His disciples that rejoicing would follow. He compared it to a woman having pain in childbirth but rejoicing in the birth of a child (John 16:20-22).

The disciples were to rely on God for strength during the transition. "For the Father Himself loves you" (v. 27). If the move really gets to you, spend more time in prayer and meditation with the Lord. This will ultimately strengthen your faith.

● If your friends decide to have a farewell reception for you, accept it as an honor. At the reception, spend time in conversation with as many people as possible. Avoid the small clique which can form around you. Keep the conversation on positive subjects and express your appreciation of what the church has meant to you over the years.

● Maintain relationships with your friends after you move. The change may have caused some rather bitter feelings which need to be dealt with. Hurts will heal if you allow them to, and keeping cordial contact with friends in your former church will help.

GUIDELINES FOR FURTHER STUDY

Role of feelings. Any time a person changes churches there is emotion. For a family going to a new home in another city, the experience may be sad but takes with it the support and well wishes of friends. When the move is made in haste brought about by a situation of tension, emotions are negative and depressing. How we deal with our feelings is often a reflection of the maturity of our Christian lives.

Must the membership be moved? I am personally hard-pressed to find formal membership in the church presented in the pages of the New Testament. Though strong discipline was exercised in the early church, membership seemed to be informal. People fellowshiped with other believers rather than joined. But because of today's culture and the general acceptance of membership, it's important to unite with another church as soon as your decision to be part of that congregation is firm. You'll find acceptance and opportunities to serve and you'll get to know people who can help you in time of need.

QUESTIONS TO ASK YOURSELF

1. Have I really explored all the avenues for making my church meaningful for me and those close to me?
2. Have I been honest with the pastor and others in the church, as well as with myself?
3. Will I have to give up too much of a doctrinal or spiritual nature to make a change?
4. Have I searched for the mind of God in the change? Do I feel that it is within His will that I find a different church in which to worship Him?
5. Am I going about a change in the right way? When I announce my action, will I keep from hurting the feelings of others? What will I say if people show that they really want me to stay? What if their feelings show they really want me to go?
6. Are my actions glorifying to God and beneficial to the church?

"May God, the source of patience and encouragement, enable you to have the same point of view among yourselves by following the example of Christ Jesus."—Romans 15:5

FOOTNOTES

CHAPTER 1
1. Donald L. Kline, "A Minister Meets Christ," *Good News*, January-February 1984, pp. 15-18.
2. Dick Innes, *I Hate Witnessing*, Vision House, Prolog.
3. Edmund Robb, Jr., "The Renewal I See in the Methodist Church," *Good News*, January-February 1984, pp. 6-12.

CHAPTER 3
1. Bruce Shelley, "Developing an Ear for Thunder," *Conservative Baptist Magazine*, Fall 1977, p. 8.
2. Clio Thomas, "We Do Worship," *Advent Christian Witness*, April, 1983, pp. 16-17.

CHAPTER 5
1. Elton Trueblood, *Company of the Committed*, Harper and Row, p. 72.
2. "What's Happening in Worship Today?" *Church of God Evangel*, February 13, 1984, p. 3.
3. Ray H. Hughes, "Pentecostal Worship," *Church of God Evangel*, February 13, 1984, p. 23.
4. Lum and Abner, Columbia Broadcasting System, March 17, 1944.
5. Lamar Vest, "Corporate Worship", *Church of God Evangel*, February 13, 1984, p. 14.

CHAPTER 6
1. "When the Pastor Gets Divorced," *Leadership*, Fall 1981, p. 19.
2. Roy C. Price, "Building Trust between Pastor and Congregation," *Leadership*, Spring 1980, p. 50.
3. Croft M. Rentz, "Longevity in the Pastorate," *Pulpit Helps*, February, 1983, p. 1.

4. "American Methodism at 200," *Christianity Today*, November 9, 1984, p. 19.
5. Paul Robbins and Harold Myra, "A Psychiatrist Looks at Troubled Pastors," *Leadership*, Spring, 1980, p. 109.
6. James L. Johnson, "The Ministry Can be Hazardous to Your Health," *Leadership*, Winter 1980, p. 34.
7. "When the Pastor Gets Divorced," *Leadership*, Fall 1981, p. 124.
8. Charles Keysor, "Life under Glass," *Christian Herald*, March 1984, p. 49.
9. James L. Johnson, *op. cit*, p. 37.
10. Roy C. Price, *op. cit.*, p. 48.
11. Quoted in the column, "In Ministry," *Good News*, January-February 1984.

CHAPTER 7
1. John R. Throop, "Leading Groups and Committees Your Way," *Innovations*, p. 28.
2. James L. Johnson, "The Ministry Can Be Hazardous to Your Health," *Leadership*, Winter 1980, p. 36.

CHAPTER 8
1. Myron Rush, *Management: A Biblical Approach*, Victor Books, 1983, pp. 212-213.

CHAPTER 9
1. *1984 Statistical Abstract of the United States.* US Department of Commerce, Bureau of Census, Washington DC.
2. Edward Dayton and Ted Engstrom, "The Challenge of the Cost," *Christian Leadership Letter*, March 1983, p. 1.
3. *Ibid.* p. 2.
4. Jack Benny, Columbia Broadcasting System, March 16, 1952.
5. Chuck Colson Interview, "Speaking Out on Fund Raising Heresy," *Christian Advertising Forum*, April-May 1983, p. 9.

CHAPTER 10
1. David Gates and Holly Morris, "Of Profits and Prophecies," *Newsweek*, December 27, 1982, p. 48.
2. Kenneth Woodward and David Gates, *Newsweek*, December 27, 1982, p. 45. (Figures on bookstores updated courtesy Christian Booksellers Assoc.)
3. News from *Religious Broadcasting*, June 1984, p. 6.
4. "Making the Bible a Living Experience," *The Pentecostal Minister*. Summer 1981, p.9.
5. John Wesley, *Sermons* vol. 1, pp. 31-32.
6. William Marty Interview, "Bible Study Doesn't Have to End When You Graduate from Moody," *Moody Alumni*, Summer 1984, pp. 5-7.
7. David Thompson, "Bible Study That Works," *Good News*, November-December 1983, p. 45.

8. John N. Oswalt, "God's Book," *Good News*, November-December, 1983, p.7.
9. Wiliam Marty, *op. cit.*, pp. 5-7.
10. "The Bible for Survival," *Good News*, November-December, 1983, p. 61.
11. "Making the Bible a Living Experience," *op. cit.*, p. 61.

CHAPTER 11
1. Russell Shive, "Are We Telling the Truth About Ourselves?" *The Link*, January 1984, p. 1.
2. Joan Martin, "What to Do with T.H.E.M." *Power for Living*, September 2, 1984, p.4.

CHAPTER 12
1. *Christianity Today*, July 13, 1984, p. 38.
2. Deborah Brunt, "What Do I Do When My Church Is Dying?" *Moody Monthly*, April 1983, p. 54.
3. Francis Schaeffer, *The Church Before the Watching World*, InterVarsity Press, p. 74.

3 1110